The Yoke
of
Perfection

by
AC Jacobs

Your Written Purpose
2017

Scripture quotations taken from The Holy Bible, New International Version® NIV ®
Copyright © 1973, 1978, 1984, 2011 by Biblica, Inc.™
Used by permission. All rights reserved worldwide.

ISBN-13: 978-0-692-90708-5 (Your Written Purpose, LLC)
ISBN-10: 0692907084

All to Jesus
I surrender
All to Him I freely give
I will ever love and trust Him
In His presence, daily live

I surrender all
I surrender all
All to thee my blessed Savior
I surrender all

Dedication

This book is dedicated to my mother,
Marilyn Ausby-Eskridge,
whose love, support, and guidance
has always mirrored that of Christ's
and has been the foundation on which I stand.

I love you, Mommy.

Acknowledgements

SENIOR YEAR of my undergraduate studies I completed an honors thesis in which I was discouraged from writing the name "Jesus" in my acknowledgements.

I did it anyway. So, in true form...

To the Captain of my ship, the Author and Finisher of my faith, my Creator, My Lord, My Savior Jesus Christ — there aren't enough words in any language that exhaustively express the gratitude and humility I feel for being chosen by you. Thank you for turning everything I've done wrong and every wrong done to me into a testament of your power and your faithfulness. Thank you for teaching me how to love myself simply because you love me. Above you there is no other name, and to your name only be all the glory, all the honor, and all the praise.

To my mother—my first friend, teacher, and love. Thank you for instilling in me a love for learning, but more importantly, thank you for teaching me about the love of

Jesus. You never claimed to be perfect nor did you allow perfection to keep you from being the best example of a woman of faith I could have ever prayed for. Thank you for every sacrifice you made to give me the best life possible. For unashamedly allowing God to lead you as the one whom He entrusted with my care, I am eternally thankful. I love you.

To my sisters—my best friends and bodyguards. I have always admired you both for living your truest, most authentic selves. Thank you for being constant examples of how to make the most out of life. Thank you for putting up with my mood swings, moments of isolation, and most importantly being there during every high and low moment of my life. God truly blessed me with the best sisters to love.

To my sons— Tacari, you've shown me the importance of forgiving myself and continuing to move forward in life. Your joy and spirit teach Mommy that life is bigger than any failure, struggle, or obstacle we can ever face. You've taught me how to fight for myself and the ones I love. I thank God daily for entrusting you in my care. You are my life's greatest gift. My little peanut, still growing in my womb — you've put a fire inside of Mommy that only your life could have done. As we grow together, I anticipate the day I can hold your face and tell you how much just knowing you are coming has changed Mommy for the better. What God has planned for your life is bigger than you and I could ever dream. My love for the you both is immeasurable.

To my husband, my life partner, the man who chose me as I was— When I married you, I knew all the feel-good reasons to love you. With you I felt safety, security, and freedom. After being married to you, I've learned that love runs much deeper than enjoying the things that feel good. Its fighting for tomorrow even when today has taken everything out of the both of us. Its looking forward to coming home to you even when we do not have any words to say. Love is proven when everything looks muddy, but finding a way to see you smile makes it all clear again. Being your wife has taught me how to love like Christ loves, and how to appreciate God's love for me. You are, still, the best thing I never knew I needed. I love you, Papa Bear.

To those of you whom have prayed for me and my life's work, I thank you for going to God on my behalf and trusting that He would hear your prayers. For carrying me to the feet of Jesus when I felt like I could not even stand. For having strong enough faith to get me from where I was to all that He has created and called me to be. It is because of your prayers that I have been able to push through.

I pray this book touches each and every one of your lives and encourages you to continue to draw closer to the Greatest Love known to man.

Love Always

AC Jacobs

Contents

Introduction

*"When people made up their minds
that they wanted to be free and took action,
then there was change."*
— Rosa Parks

What is yoke? Dictionary.com defines yoke as, "a wooden crosspiece that is fastened over the neck of two animals and attached to the plow or cart that they are to pull", synonymous with "harness, collar, coupling". Webster defines yoke as, "a frame fitted to a person's shoulders to carry a load in two equal portions." The Bible defines yoke as staff, or bar, both used figuratively to denote severe bondage, affliction, or subjection. Why would I, then, call perfection a yoke. Surely, I am not claiming to walk around with a physical yoke, because those are made for animals, right? I am glad you asked.

Evidence of United States history shows us that these contraptions, designed for animals, were used on the enslaved Africans as a mechanism to, for lack of better words, "keep them in line." This yoke served as a tool to benefit the slave masters to control the physical body of the enslaved. But the control of that yoke was far more destructive than that of simply the physical. The psychological, mental, emotional, spiritual, and familial break down of the enslaved holds a lasting effect, even until today. If you can imagine for one minute, not just your hands and feet shackled in chains, but your neck. You cannot look left, right, back, or up. You can only see that which fits into your peripheral view, that which is beneath you, and that which is in front of you—this case being another human being whose posture mirrored yours. The constant visual placed in your mind is bondage and the inability to break free, even of the way you see your life.

Most of us have never been in that type of life circumstance. What we know of slavery is limited to the numerous movies produced that can only attempt to portray what life must really have been like. With the exception of the millions of men and women incarcerated, most of us will never know what it feels like to physically have our hands tied up, let alone our feet and necks. That material yoke is not how we are still enslaved. It is the invisible yokes, most times the ones we choose, that keep us with the visual of constant bondage with no way toward freedom.

This book was given to me when everything I had done in the natural had proven to be ineffective. I went to college and studied the craft of creative writing. I went on to further pursue my writing at the graduate level under the tutelage of remarkable writers, completed the novel that had been burning inside of me, then placed it in my desk. Even throughout my schooling, I was always told that I needed a job to fund my passion. Being an artist is far from cheap. It was no surprise, then, that when the opportunity for a full-time position, with benefits, became available to me I jumped without hesitation.

I was in my last semester of graduate school, I had just gotten married, and earlier in that year, my husband purchased us a home. That year was full of great and wonderful happenings—all things I had prayed for my entire life. I was beyond grateful. I was also, however, on my way to being exhausted and empty, without paying any attention. Needless to say, once life slowed down, I realized some changes beginning to take place that were never intended to promote the gift God had given me. To begin with, I stayed at a job where I knew my integrity would soon be in question out of fear of not having a paycheck. This job drained so much out of me I didn't have energy or time for the things that mattered most like, my new husband, my family, my writing, and most importantly, my relationship with Christ.

Today's culture over glorifies being busy and not having time to do anything. It is almost as if there is a secret reward for being "#teamnosleep". Everybody is hustling and waking up early to catch the worms. And that's a good thing! At least people aren't glorifying laying on the couch all day. But there is a benefit in knowing that rest and prioritization are important elements to a healthy life. And if we are always busy, yet remaining empty and stagnant, why are we busy?

Rest—I hardly had any of that. I do not mean sleep, I mean rest. My brain was forever turning flips trying to figure out how I had gotten myself into such an emotionally abusive work situation at the "highest point" in my life. I was working my butt off—many times beyond the allocated work hours—and still, at times, could not afford gas to get to work. If there was any luxury (anything outside of the necessary bills) I had given it up. Which was a sacrifice I was willing to make. But when I saw my nature beginning to change and thus the nature of those who meant the world to me change as a result—that was not something I was willing to sacrifice.

So, I left. Things were going to get better, right?

False.

If we aren't careful, we will fall into the trap of making decisions at the height of our emotional connection to them. Did I need to leave? Yes. Was I ready to leave? Physically, yes. Was I prepared for what would come once we now had to live off one income with no certainty when I would find a permanent job? Was I prepared for my decision to affect the people I loved the most? Was I prepared to live out the age old saying, "the Lord will provide"? In theory, yes. Did I believe God had okayed my leave? Yes. Had I slowed down to ask Him any other questions? Did I pause? Did I ask for clarity? Or had I developed the mindset that when faced with less than ideal situations, you run because there is no way perfection can be attained there, anyway…

The hard reality about listening to God is that you must follow through. Half obedience is not obedience at all. In the same sense that James says, "faith by itself, if it is not accompanied by action, is dead (James 2:17 NIV)", you cannot take part of God's word to you and choose which part to obey. I left that job. I knew I had something coming up that would make ends meet, but He gave me an assignment to complete and my emotions, my feelings, and my inability to control them made me incapable of completing it. Like the good Father He is, He kept me, covered me, and blessed me, in spite of. But like the good Father He is, He corrected me and allowed test and trial after test and trial to sharpen me into a whole person, not just a well person.

This book should have been written years ago. At least, I was to have been writing, fervently, years ago, when I left that job. But I wasn't strong enough—I didn't know that I was strong enough—to overcome the on-slaught of emotions that manifested with this experience. If there were ever a time I was depressed with life, it was then. I had many heartbreaks and disappointments in life, but the feeling of depression only came when I reached the end of my own abilities and lost sight of who enabled me to have them in the first place. To unpack the last statement, you will have to keep reading, because you cannot appreciate your ending without understanding your beginning.

Had I ever been able to deal with my emotions? Had I ever misused a blessing? Had I ever listened to God and experienced more immediate pain than pleasure? Was it just that moment? That incident? Or was this a habit? Did I know what to do once something I thought came from God fell apart? Could I maintain my character when my circumstances did not fit my desires?

I claimed freedom in Christ but wore an invisible yoke, every day of my life. Not just when I graduated and my adult life went into full swing. I'd worn this yoke for as long as my memory allows me to recall.

But thank God for Jesus.

I began writing this book with a specific audience—the young, Black, educated, Christian woman searching for a safe place to be all that makes her unique. Yet as paragraphs turned into pages, and pages into chapters, I realized that though my experience may speak directly to that demographic, God can use our struggles and victories for those who do fall into their own unique characterizations. Besides, if you are not the young, Black, educated, Christian woman, chances are you are in close proximity to one or your life has been touched by one. Women who fit those specifications are the trailblazers of this generation, and whether the world likes it or not, we are not going anywhere.

All of the various aspects that make up our identities play significant roles in shaping each of us into the person we are to be. With every change of season comes a new role. If we are not careful, the expectations of what is supposed to be instead of what is will quickly change joy and freedom to despair and sorrow. Instead of embracing the different roles, we become enslaved to the worldly expectations attached to them. As you read through this book, I pray God reveals anything in your life that would keep you from living in His freedom. May you find rest and peace in His strength and allow the yokes to be released.

Here we go.

Perfection (n.) — per|fec|tion

1. The quality or state of being perfect: such as
    a. Freedom from fault or defect: flawlessness
    b. MATURITY
    c. The quality or state of being saintly

2. An exemplification of supreme excellence
    a. An unsurpassable degree of accuracy or
       excellence

3. The act or process of perfecting

The Picture
of Perfection

> - *"Ms. Third Ward, what is your aspiration in life?"*
> - *"My aspiration in life? To be happy."*
> — Beyoncé, Pretty Hurts (music video)

Of the time I have been alive, there is one entertainer who stands out high above the rest. Most all polls would agree that Beyoncé Knowles-Carter is this generation's greatest performer/entertainer, though there are several people who also believe she is overrated, especially other entertainers. In any case, Beyoncé has made herself a brand that seems nearly untouchable. Beyond her music, Beyoncé has become an icon for people all around the world. She has gained the loyalty and die-hard support of people she will never meet, but whose lives she has obviously deeply touched. Her fan base, most notably referred to as the "Beyhive", behaves unlike any other fan base you will

9

ever encounter; from defending Beyoncé against her critics to nearly (and only nearly because the two are still happily married) threatening Jay-Z's life over what most people believed to be her alleged confession of his infidelity with the release of her latest album, "Lemonade".

Though I do not prescribe myself to the Beyhive, I have been a fan of Beyoncé since her early days in Destiny's Child and willingly admit that as I experienced life, I have consistently listened to Beyoncé's music through the best and worst times. But as I mentioned before, Beyoncé is not just praised for her music. Anything she does is deemed noteworthy—from wearing a $23 t-shirt or attending dinner for a best friend. Her security is probably the best security anyone can afford. She hardly speaks to the media, almost always wears a smile, and tries consistently to support and uplift disenfranchised groups. Her life, her career, her marriage—SHE—is idolized by young babies up to seasoned adults. Yet even Beyoncé will admit that perfection, the quest for it, and the gravitational pull of it, is crippling to us as a people. On her self-titled album BEYONCÉ, one of her more famous tracks is, *Flawless*. Women all over the world began to brag about the flawlessness of their own nature and everything else about them as individuals. In a sense, she boosted the self-esteem of women who otherwise suffered, and even that of those who could use a dose of humility. But there is another track she released as a single that holds more truth than maybe any other songs of that album: *Pretty Hurts*.

To grasp a full understanding of the magnitude of the importance of this song it must be combined with the video representation she released. The scene is a beauty pageant: on stage, backstage, preparation, home shrine of trophies won. Images of women competing with each other flash across the screen: fighting for blow dryers, sabotaging each other's costumes, side-eyeing each other's every move. You'll see Beyoncé putting Vaseline on her teeth to keep her smile, leaning over a toilet to lose a little extra weight, and nervously stepping on to a scale and having her body measurements taken. Other participants pinch the "loose" skin on their bodies, pack on pounds of make-up, all in search of PERFECTION. The singer calls perfection the disease of a nation, something which we try to fix outwardly but are unable to because it comes from the inside.

Now for every person who adores Beyoncé, there is another who could care less about the air she breathes. Whether lyrically, vocally, socially, any other-ly, people have their opinions about her as a person and a performer. Whatever your opinion might be, though, I hope you find the true significance of this generation having a song like this, especially coming from someone with such an influence as Mrs. Carter. While many would say that she has the *perfect* life, of the many songs she sings, this is one she actually wrote as well. What that says to me is that this is a concern of hers, a matter that is pressing on her heart enough to put pen to paper, mouth to mic, and face to screen. Because she has become an idol, many people forget that she is human. Idols are perfect, incapable of ever falling. At least that is what we require of them. But before they become idols, they are human, just like us. They have families, feelings, and have to make choices and deal with the consequence of those choices like normal people. I believe that even with all the worldly success she has acquired, *Pretty Hurts* is a testament to the harsh realities of living a life such as hers. The constant spotlight and pressure to fit the world's idea of perfection is not just exhausting, but also unhealthy and even debilitating.

Perfection *is* the disease of a nation—America being the first in line. From the influx of social media avenues and its accessibility for any one of any age, the pressure to appear perfect or completely put together is unsurmountable. When I was 12, it was enough pressure trying to run four laps around the PE Campus on lap day, remember to take my PE clothes home that day and bring them back on Monday. Yes, there were still the natural pressures of who wants to be your friend and when will the boys like me, but that is pretty common across generations. Children growing up today are exposed to more information than we can accurately measure. I cannot imagine having to make sense of the world the way kids do now because it is all way too much and way too fast. Twelve-year-olds feel like they need to have the same things thirty-year-olds do, and fifty-year-olds are still crying about not looking thirty anymore. Thirty-year-olds and almost thirty-year-olds, meanwhile, are just smiling through their realities because let's face it, "adult-ing" is hard (this is a generalization—I know that everyone is not facing these problems). The point is, everyone is looking at someone else to make sense of themselves. Though this song and video is centered around outward beauty, the message is still pertinent for all realms of life.

Most of us are suffering from something on the inside that we cannot see or fix, so we place our focus on outward things like, beauty, clothes, cars, careers, husbands, kids, hobbies. You name it, there is someone struggling with that. But all of those things are cover-ups for insecurities we do not know how to deal with.

My biggest insecurity? Take a wild guess. Yup. Perfection. What particular strand? Well, several, actually.

- I have a hard time telling people no.
- I want to fix everyone's problems.
- I do not like when people are mad at me.
- I trust myself to get things done better than others.
- I think about the decisions I make so I feel as if people need to not have their opinions (or at least not share them) and trust that I know what I am doing (especially about my child).
- I do not know how to ask for help—in fact, I become anxious when I know that I have no other option but to ask for help.

And these are just a few areas. My need for things to be perfect, to my understanding of perfection, continue to reveal themselves for me the older I get. Some of you might be wondering, "What's wrong with striving for perfection? Isn't that what we all should want? Aren't you Christians supposed to perfect?" Make it through to the end of this book and I will answer these questions for you, especially the last one.

There's nothing wrong with trying to reach a whole, well, healthy, happy, and full version of ourselves. We can strive to perform our best at work, in our families, and with our friends by setting goals and reaching them. We can, and we should, eliminate the things in our lives that hurt us, hinder us, cause us to do those things to ourselves and keep us from being our best selves. But we must first be honest about what those things are. In striving for the worldly concept of perfection, we set ourselves up for failure. How? Everyone has a different idea of perfection.

For example, what one mother believes is the perfect way to raise children, another will believe is totally wrong. The hardest lesson in perfection I have had to learn was that of being a mother to my son. Naturally, mothers want what is best for their children and as the vehicle through which that child is formed and birthed into the world, we have the responsibility of raising them the best we can. But it is easy to fall into the trap of perfection with all the opinions about motherhood. Natural birth or c-section? Home delivery or hospital? Breast milk or formula? Cloth diapers or store bought? Freshly made or jar food? How early do you let them leave the house? How early do you leave the house? Who can hold your baby? Who can watch your baby? Stay-at-home or daycare? Honestly, this list could go on and on and never stop because as times change, so do the opinions of people and that with which we choose to consume our time. I actually thought I had recovered from my perfectionist tendencies, but becoming a mother showed me just how deep that pressing desire ran in my veins. If there is any life lesson that will teach you imperfection, it is parenthood. And not because you are a bad parent, but because there is no humanly possible way to control everything babies and children do.

My style of parenting falls on the cautious and conservative side. Even now as my son is getting older and getting into anything he can get his hands on, I have a difficult time dealing with, "He's a boy. They are going to hurt themselves." Though I say it to myself and reassure my husband when needed, inside I feel, "How can you let that happen to your baby?" Every time he has fallen, bumped his head, smashed his own fingers with his toys, I feel a level of guilt that is not as easy to shake with, "things are going to happen." And as if that guilt is not enough, I nearly lose my entire mind when his "accident" happens because of me. The process usually goes like this:

1. Make sure he's okay
2. Immediate guilt and shame
3. Figure out how much care will he need right now and later
4. Protect yourself from what other people will say/have said about you
5. Keep going

It is the last two points that happen hand in hand and drain me of any and every ounce of energy I have left after chasing behind my baby who has by this time forgotten whatever happened to him and showered me with more hugs and kisses than I can number. Though he still calls and cries for me, I am still crying internally, not just because I "allowed" something to hurt him, but because I know I will face the judgment of others because of it. It is a constant pull of "you are equipped to take care of this child" and "maybe you're not as cut out for this mom thing as you think."

How, then, can I be of any good to my child when my mind is torn into two extremes? A paraphrase of James 1:8 says that a double-minded man is unstable in all his ways. How can I be both bound to this notion that everything must be perfect yet clearly unstable? Instability cannot breed perfection and perfection cannot breed instability.

This is where perfection becomes my yoke. I start to think about all the ways in which this incident can change the way I think about myself and how others view me as well. I shame myself for falling short. I punish myself for not being able to keep him away from anything that can hurt him. I listen to the opinions of other people who obviously would never be able to make the same mistakes because, clearly, they are the perfect ones and not me. I become more careful. More cautious. More conservative. I strip myself of the right to forgive. I cripple myself from moving past the situation once it is over. I look for other people to affirm me. I look for other people to tell me it is not my fault and he will be ok. I pour more of me into my child, and less into anything else. Still, it is not enough. People still talk, the shame doesn't disappear, but time moves on, and so must I.

Earlier I posed a hypothetical question concerning Christians and perfection. Perhaps the notion that Jesus Christ is perfect and we follow him is the beginning place of the myth that Christian believers are perfect people, or at least they should be. After all, Matthew 5:48 reads, "Be perfect, therefore as your heavenly Father is perfect (NIV)." But I would argue that God's perfection has little to do with such thinking. I believe that the idea of a perfect Christian originated when Christianity became more religion than relationship, and the work of Jesus was forgotten because of the works of man. When "Christians" shifted the focus from the redemptive power of the blood of Jesus and his resurrection and replaced it with "but we go to church every Sunday, and we do not smoke, drink, curse, gamble, lie, cheat, steal, eat pork" and so forth and so on, even that which Jesus commanded in Matthew 5:48 became diluted and misinterpreted for the sake of man's own gain.

As I have embarked on my own journey to find God, live in His truth and understand His Word, I have found that much of what has been taught in Christian circles has not been complete, or whole. Not necessarily all wrong, though some teachings have been flat out like, "what Bible did that come from?" I mean, let's face it; America was created on the backs of enslaved African peoples and nourished with their blood and tears for over 400 years, and is still legally benefitting from the abuse of power of those in leadership and administration. The lack of careful attention given to proper interpretation has given people the room to read scripture from a world view instead of a biblical view.

We see this in the case of perfection in Matthew 5:48, but we see it in simpler terms like "disciple" in Matthew 5:3.

Verse 48 ends Matthew chapter 5, but from verses 3-48, Jesus is teaching his disciples how they are to live. Before Jesus' death, disciple meant, "a learner," or, "pupil." In some cases, the term is used concerning the twelve Jesus called to follow him, in others the term is used to refer to pupils of John the Baptist or even the Pharisees. But a disciple simply was one who followed and learned the teachings of their teacher. Different scholars argue on whether not the disciples referred to in Matthew 5:48 are exclusive to the twelve or if "disciples" included the multitudes that had begun to follow Jesus as a result of his teaching, preaching, and miracles. This distinction matters when a group of people try to tell you that Jesus only came to save them and not you, and you, therefore, cannot be a recipient of His love, grace, and gift of eternal life. If Jesus was only speaking to the twelve, how can the multitudes know what was expected of them as followers of Christ? Could the others ever be considered followers of Christ? This is where confusion begins.

We know that the term "disciple" took on a much broader meaning after Jesus' death. After Jesus died and rose again, it is safe to replace the term *disciple* with *Christian*. Why is that? Because if what makes us a believer is the acceptance of Jesus' virgin birth, death, burial, resurrection, and promise to return again, then those of us who have made that profession and had a true conversion of our hearts are adopted into the family of Christ. We have become God's children as joint heirs with Christ (Romans 8:17). As God's children, we are mandated to share that good news with the world. If we believe John 3:16, that God loved the *world*, then we believe He did not just want to save you and me, He came to save the *world*. If we believe that Jesus planned to save the Gentiles as well as the Jews, and that we all would be one family (Ephesians 3:6), then we would thank God for His love and grace and share it with the *world*. We would live out the entirety of Matthew 28:19-20, going out to teach *all nations* the things which Jesus commanded. If we believe that God shows no favoritism (Romans 2:11), then we should do the same. Any teaching that has come from "the church" or even claims from the Bible that elevate one group of people over the others is a distortion and misinterpreted view of the fullness of God. For this reason, America is plagued with a disease of racism that not only separates us but binds us to un-forgiveness, unrepentance, and the inability to heal from our past. The struggle is and has been that most racist and separatist ideologies have been "supported" with scripture.

If the misinterpretation of a word as simple as disciple has created entire factions and sects of "bible based beliefs" enough to rotten an entire nation, what can we expect with a word that holds as much weight as perfection? One of the things I love about the word of God is that even when something seems difficult to understand, God has already provided us with clarification. This same story told in Matthew 5 is also recorded in Luke 6. What Matthew records in 5:48 reads, "Be perfect, therefore, as your Heavenly Father is perfect." Luke 6:36, which marks the same spot in Jesus' teaching as Matthew 5:48 (you should read both on your own so that you may see for yourself) reads, "Be merciful, just as your Father is merciful." Now some critics and skeptics would call this an "inconsistency" because how can the same story be told two different ways if it were true? As believers who rely on the Holy Spirit to reveal the truth of God's inspired word and as students of the word, we know this is not an inconsistency but a revelation of what God truly intended for us to grasp. We see that what Matthew calls perfection, Luke calls merciful. What then is Jesus teaching? When you read both of these chapters in their entirety, Jesus is teaching how to live out that which is on the inside of God's heart for His people. He is teaching his followers how to love to each other and those we would call our "enemies" as He shows love to us. He is teaching, essentially, how to mirror His own life—complete and whole, and morally and ethically just.

Sinless-ness and perfection are characteristics of God reserved for God. Mankind cannot ever be God and thus cannot achieve what our minds perceive to be perfection. We have ideas of perfect weather, perfect dates, perfect weddings. What we mean and expect of perfection is absolutely no fault, no wrong, and the inability to become any better. But if we learn to see Biblical perfection as a mandate to imitate the ways of the Father, we will know that we are made perfect (whole, complete, holy, and just) because He has given us grace through the death and resurrection of Jesus Christ. We are made perfect as we live in Him and through

Him and are transformed to be like Him in our everyday lives. God knows that we will fall short—He is not expecting anything otherwise. What He does desire, however, is that as we mimic the example He gave us (in Jesus), our hearts and attitudes about our shortcomings, and those of others begins to change. "People look at outer appearance, but the Lord looks at the heart (Samuel 16:7, NIV)."

But that is not what we have been taught.

Perfection has been equated to supremacy: racial supremacy, gender supremacy, class supremacy. We have taken what God intended to unify us and used it as a way to further separate ourselves from each other. If it is not by race, it is by class. If it is not by either of those, it is by gender. And it is not by any of those, it is by which sins we commit and which ones "them over there" commit. Everyone is searching for a way to make it to the top (which is what religions try to provide—a moral ladder to perfection) when Christians have the unique reality that He who was on top came down to us without us having to fix one thing. He offered His perfect life in exchange for ours so that we may be in communion again with our Creator. Yet we are consistently searching for validation and purpose in the things of the world.

Christians seem to be just as, if not more, hopeless than those who do not know Christ. And it is because we have not allowed Him complete control in the act of surrender. When we surrender our problems, our insecurities, our shortcomings and failures, our sins, our past, our hurt, our pain, God turns it around and uses it for His glory, to draw more people to Him.

But we try to fix everything on our own.

If you aren't the perfectionist this book is speaking to, you're in close proximity to one and the side effects are contagious.

I mentioned a few ways in which I have suffered from my yoke of perfection. Those are ways in which I personally have had difficulty allowing God to be God, and people to be all that God has created them to be. But perfectionism is not limited to a person who has to have all things around them perfect. No, quite the contrary. Perfectionism is so subtle and slick, it surrounds us in the simplest forms and we do not even recognize it. Envy—side effect of perfection. Jealousy—Side effect. Self-hate, self-righteousness, depression, coveted-ness, weight issues, bitterness, despair. Do you see where I am going? The world has created such a platform for us to compare ourselves against it that we have forgotten who made the world and everyone and everything in it.

A very special person in my life sat down and spoke with me about the way in which society has made her hate just about everything about herself. As a young Black girl who attended a predominantly non-black school, the images around her made her question, "why am I just brown, everything?" Brown skin, brown hair, brown eyes. She recalled how the other girls at school had different shades of eye colors, various textures and shades of hair and skin tones. She always felt plain, regular, and not special. As a fan of Barbie, she also could not understand why her body was not shaped like that of the doll or her other friends, either. The comments made by the girls she thought were here friends and the images she saw on both TV and in her toys made her feel like, "why am I just Black?" One "Heritage Day" at school, all the kids began sharing their ethnic make-up. Hardly any only named one group. By the time it was her turn, she told her class her father was French, because she did not want to be the only person who was "just Black."

The insecurities about her skin, hair, and weight eventually led to an eating disorder for which she needed extended medical treatment. She courageously shared that the disorder had so much control over her mind, she would see the number of calories of any food flash across her head before she considered eating it. Frequent visits to the scale affirmed her as she saw pounds drop, dramatically. But more than anything, the responses she received from so-called friends and even family members translated to, "they like me better now." Comments that suggested modeling, or even praised her *now* "beautiful brown skin" gave her the temporary satisfaction of others approval. But even as she received all the praise, she did not know where, or even how, to stop. I said early that there is no way we can understand the pressure children of today are facing, and this is one example of what I mean. A beautiful girl, inside and out, became so lost in what she wasn't, she did not know how to love everything she was.

I asked her what changed, what helped her begin to see her own worth and beauty. To my surprise, she responded, "when Whitney Houston died, I started looking up her music and pictures and I thought, 'Wow, she was so beautiful.'" She was too young to really know a well, healthy,

Whitney Houston so as she discovered the Whitney that everyone older than her was mourning, for the first time she thought, "Black is beautiful." The process of her healing would begin, but it would undoubtedly take time.

As women of color, right now is the best time to love and appreciate exactly how God made you. There is an on-slaught of positive reinforcement, most notably identified as #blackgirlmagic, and it is not exclusive to any skin tone, hair texture, weight, or size.

Or is it? Is the trendy #BlackGirlMagic only reserved for the ones who are bold enough to accept themselves, flaws and all? Is it reserved for the social elite who are handed passes from society to live freely anyway? Is the girl who still struggles with accepting her dark skin falling for the "magic" being proclaimed by the girl whose daddy is white? Is the "natural" curly-headed-girl actually inspiring the "natural" low-cut-girl? Are the women who fall under the "conventional definitions" of beauty making a dent in the issues that girls who aren't are facing? For every advance in healing, there is still a scar, for someone, that convinces them, "but that's *STILL* not for you."

Our identity, one of the most important aspect of our lives, is wrapped in what society and culture tells us we are, instead of who God has told us we are. Women. Black women. Black educated women (and by educated, I mean any woman who has ever picked up a book, watched the news, or simply lived life—not all education come from the school system). Black educated women who still love Jesus—we simply do not make sense to the world. The world teaches that Jesus belongs to the white man. Our education teaches us that we have been at the center of every fight for justice though dismissed and neglected in the history books, even our own. Our race and culture often makes us choose whether we are first Black, or woman. And our gender, well, we still have to fight to prove that we are, too, women.

We attempt to live freely, but we are faced with the limitations that come from worldly expectations. We fight for women's right, we support and fight for our Black men, we earn degrees upon degrees upon degrees, and we keep our faith even when everything around us suggests letting it all go.

Because at the end of every day, all we really have is Jesus. Not the religion. Not the culture. Not the degrees. Not the solidarity of other women. The relationship with Jesus.

That used to be hard for me. I didn't want to be one of 'those crazy Jesus people." I wanted people to understand that I understood them. I did not want people to think, "all she's gonna do is tell me about Jesus, again." But through it all, it is the grounding and foundation of His love reflected in me that made anything I've ever done possible. I wanted to rely on the things about me that would not make people uncomfortable. I wanted to always be someone everyone would like. I wanted to create my ball of perfection, make myself untouchable, and live my life, *happily*.

I began this chapter with an epigraph from the music video for Beyoncé's, *Pretty Hurts*. At the root of the need for perfection is the desire to be happy. Continuously happy. For ourselves, and for the people we love. It is the ways in which we strive to obtain that happiness that lead us into the trap of fitting the world's definition of perfection.

But, we do not have to carry that weight anymore.

It is time to unpack.

2

The **Practice**
of Perfection

"Tell the truth and shame the devil"
— African American Aphorism

I was in the third grade when I received my first B. I am not sure how many people remember report cards, but I do. They all looked the same up until that point. Straight As and Es (for excellent), because I knew better to act up in class, too. The smile that lit up my mother's face was what I told myself was the reason I tried so hard for good grades. I was not always honest enough to admit that receiving $20 for each A at such a young age had anything to do with it. Even further, I had not learned how to be real with myself—being a good student was all I believed I was good at. I remember being complimented for being "good", and "so smart". I was shy, quiet, and preferred to be alone rather than in big groups or crowds. I liked books, high heels and purses, but I also loved playing football with the boys—grass or concrete. It didn't matter. Early on I developed a complex of never being girly enough to be the girl boys liked nor fully a tomboy because I loved being a girl. Even innocent elementary flirtation was always backed with some notion of being everybody's friend.

My older sister never had this problem. Being just a year and a half a part, we spent the beginning of our schooling years in the same schools. Boys always liked her and for as long as I've known her, she could care less about flowers, the color pink, or any other stereotypical girl thing. In fact, she was one of the boys more than I ever was. My younger sister would not have this problem, either. She, too, a Brainiac on her own merit, was never really much into the girly things, except for when she began designing and making clothes out of paper. We all had an affinity for sports, maybe because my dad did not have any boys, but my sisters possessed something from the early ages that I had to learn and develop.

What I have grown to understand about my sisters and myself was that they never cared what people had to think of them. They are, now, have been, and will always be themselves. I did not really know what that meant for me. I didn't fit in to any one category except I had a big brain that showed up and performed well in academic setting. In kindergarten, my teacher Ms. Little would give me the 1st grade vocabulary because I was too advanced for the work she had given the rest of my class. At my first elementary school, I was always in a blended class with the grade right above me. My first and second grade teacher, Ms. Burke, called on me for everything, especially reading out loud. When I switched elementary schools because my current one was closing, I was placed in the blended 4th and 5th grade class where my teacher, Mr. Cuba, sighed breaths of release to have me—and one other student, Do (pronounced Doe--he was a fifth grader and my competition) in his class. He didn't have to raise his voice or even repeat himself. Sometimes, maybe for his own humor, I can never be sure, he would ask questions that Do and I would go back and forth about. We could never be on the same team during class competitions because the class always said it would be unfair. I am saying all this to say, school was never an issue for me.

But that first B shattered my eight-year-old world. I had received second and third place before in my school's "Mini-Olympics" by stopping at the finish line because I saw my mom stopped running with me on the side line. I'd embarrassed myself at a spelling bee listening to a boy tell me how to spell "totally" wrong—more on this later. But there was something heartbreaking about that B. I remember crying in my dad's stomach as he and my older sister laughed and kept telling me to stop crying, it was just a B. I wanted my Mommy because I knew she would not laugh at me, but I was also glad my dad was there for the conference because I didn't want to disappoint my mom. This is not to say that my mom would have been disappointed—this is to show you the way I thought. When we sat in front of my teacher, Ms. Wilkes, she explained to my dad that I need to work on my penmanship. Penmanship? I got a B because my handwriting needed to improve? I went from being sad to being mad. Did I score well on my tests, quizzes, and homework? Did I really deserve a B?

If I had known the practice of being honest then, I would not have even cried because I would have admitted that being a teacher's pet had its perks. Like when she could not decide who a no-name paper belonged to but she assumed it was mine because I always did my work and the other student didn't? I knew that assignment wasn't mine, but it kept me from having to sit on the bench. Years later, and maybe even that day, I felt guilty because that boy did his work and I took credit for it, but then, my only concern was keeping up with this persona of a perfect student. By any means necessary, apparently. I remember that boy despising me every time I was awarded for anything after that. Years down the line, I saw him in college, at my college, and I didn't feel so bad anymore. I was glad to see he had made it into the same university I had even though I stole his third-grade homework assignment. I do not know what kind of trouble that boy got in because of that, but I know the memory of what I did never left me and that, I hoped, would be payback enough.

I was mad at my teacher. She was one of my favorite teacher's, too. As we left the conference and went straight to basketball practice (my dad was my coach) I do not even remember practicing. Whether my dad didn't let me or I was too in my emotions, I cannot be sure. But I did not practice. Not that it mattered much. Being the coach's daughter provided NO PRIVILEGES for me. I was only good for defense at that age because what I inherited from my father was his physical strength and athletic build. That could not be taught, anyway. I went home, still crying, not wanting to show my mom my B. What did I think was going to happen? My mom wasn't a yeller, it is not like I had an F. I wasn't going to be whooped. What was I afraid of?

As an adult, I have truly wished I could erase those memories because they seem so meaningless yet they appear so vividly. Why couldn't I be like the rest of the kids who cheated in school and were happy about it because it got them to graduation? Why couldn't I be happy about a B and just strive to get an A the next time? Why can't I be like most adults and forget 99% of what happened in elementary school? Why couldn't I soothe myself with memories of how many times I let people copy my homework, classwork, and even my tests? Because receiving a perfect report card was the beginning of quest for worldly perfection. I am quite positive I single-handedly "helped" a few people graduate from middle school and high school. But the only thing I can vividly remember is the one time I cheated.

Hear me out, striving for academic excellence is admirable, and the way I grew up, expected. I still cringe when I receive Bs. The difference now is, I know that if I get a B, I earned a B. I must accept that. Now, if I truly believed I earned an A, I would fight for it. But most times, I know what I have done. Back then, I felt I deserved As. I was a good student, that should have been all that mattered. Give me my A and let me be.

Life doesn't work that way. Better yet, even when I did deserve an A, life still would not always work out in my favor. I have had to accept Bs when I knew I gave A work at times when other areas of my integrity would come into question. In God's eyes, then, I passed the real test and that is what I have come to understand is what really matters. This lesson would be one I would have to learn in several arenas of my life. But for being 8 years old, I thank God for his mercy and that He saved those lessons until I was mature enough to handle them.

Many of you might be reading and thinking, "she's tripping over a third-grade homework assignment and grade?" The answer is, yes. Because I knew better. But deep within me was a tug that would not allow me to not attain perfection at the academic level. Such perfection led me to push aside my integrity and a friendship. The reason I could not shake it is because it formed the yoke I wrote about earlier. I would have my integrity checked time and time again. When I was 8, it was over a homework assignment. When I was 14, it was over having a "boyfriend" even when my mom hadn't allowed me to start dating. When I was 17 it was about what I would be doing with and for that boyfriend without being under a microscope. When I was 20, it was about maintaining a friendship with a person who had done no wrong to me, but was rejected by the people who I wanted—needed—to accept me.

See the point is, if we do not deal with our problems, if we do not face our weaknesses, if we continue to idolize worldly achievements and accolades, we will never be free.

Perfection is my weakness. As much as I want to be rid of this incessant desire to have everything "perfect", and although I have allowed for God to release me from its control, it manifests itself in new ways as life continues and new situations occur. What takes you out of your character? What controls you to the point of making decisions you would not normally make? What has power over you, even if you do not want it to? Some of us deal with our "invisible" yokes more publicly because they manifest themselves in the forms of addictions that everyone can see. Whether its drugs, alcohol, cigarettes, the constant need to have a man—some of us cannot hide that with which we struggle. Then there are those of us who think we are getting by because what we struggle with is done behind closed doors.

In high school, a girl told me, "good girls are just bad girls who don't get caught." I am pretty sure I just called her a hater at that point, but I never forgot what she said, because I did not understand why she said it to me. Better yet, I did not like that she said it to me. Did she know something about me that I didn't know she knew? How much did she know? I also thought, no matter what she thinks she knows, I am still not as bad as her.

The recent shift from respectability politics to "no slut shaming" has a lot to do with what that girl said to me. We all have secrets, and we all have vices. But when we magnify the faults of others without acknowledging our own, we make room for people to feel condemned and judged without ever offering an opportunity for grace. Those feelings turn into defense mechanisms that prevent us from finding the root of the problem.

When I think about the compassion Jesus showed to the Samaritan woman in John 4, I am convicted, and then concerned. Especially in the church scene, sermons have been preached and scriptures have been studied, but the first word members hear of someone divorcing, or re-marrying, or entertaining a man who belongs to someone else, the response is to condemn. On the other hand, our culture has become so politically correct and afraid to tell the truth that instead of condemnation, its, "well, we do not know her story," and nothing is said, at all. Jesus gave us a clear example of how to correct someone with love, and it involves neither condemnation nor dismissal of the behaviors, and He knew her whole story. When Jesus began speaking with the Samaritan woman, He did not point out her sin, He pointed out her need. She confessed her sin and then he provided what she needed (John 4:7-26).

I question, that as women have become more and more willing to behave like men, is it because we have always been condemned without receiving compassion, or mercy? Is it because the church told us we had to be virgins while they let the boys run around because "boys will be boys?" Has our newfound freedom in sexual politics given us a Band-Aid to cover the wounds of loneliness, low self-esteem, abandonment, lack of faith, lack of trust, and oppression? I am in no way denying that women are sexual beings and only men have sexual desires. I am challenging the idea that sexual freedom equates to a lack of sexual control or restraint. For every girl who freely chose sex, whether casual or in the constraints of a relationship, there is another girl who felt some sense of guilt and shame. Whether it was because waiting for marriage had been her desire, or because that first boy treated her like a dog and left after he got his treat, there are girls, and even grown women, who have never dealt with what the loss of her virginity actually meant.

Growing up I heard over and over, "you can't miss something you never had." While I understand the premise, it is simply not enough in trying to teach a young lady the importance of chastity. Curiosity alone negates that statement. I also heard that saving yourself was important so that you may present yourself as a gift to your husband on your wedding night. Again, I get the premise, but what does this mean for the woman? What does this teach us about the faith we claim to believe?

Let me be extremely clear, I believe God made man and woman with specific and unique qualities, enough to provide distinction between man and woman. I do not believe, however, that God has a moral list of standards that apply to women and a completely different set for men. Most people completely tune out of sermons, or skip ahead a few pages in a book, when the topic of sex is discussed because so many of us are not willing to let go of it or admit it is control over our lives.

But for those of you still reading…

Every sexual encounter is a soul tie. Whether we consider the choice an accident or we truly, deeply cared about
the person with whom we chose to have sex with, a part of
us becomes a part of them, and vice versa. This is why virginity preached to women, and not men, has always been an
issue for me. As men, traditionally, are more likely to have a
larger number of sexual partners, why, then, does he get to
receive my virginity as his gift? The lopsided teaching that
has come from our pulpits and our homes—because let's be
honest, what parent is as upset about their son having sex as
they are about their daughters? Not many—has blinded us to
the beauty and sanctity of what God intended for His people.
We have made it up in our own minds that waiting is simply
too hard: "Everybody else has done it, so who else would be
a virgin like me?" In our finite minds, we decide that because
other people had sex before marriage, and God still loves
them, then we can do the same thing.

As the church, as parents, older siblings, cousins, and
friends, we've dropped the ball on teaching what is most important—obedience to God. It is not that God wants us to be
void of sexual feelings. It is not that He doesn't want you to
enjoy life. His desire is to bless and sanctify the unity of one
man and one woman as a testament of His love for the
church. The Bible portrays Jesus as the groom and the church
as His bride (Ephesians 5:22-33). Most of us can grasp that
God is a jealous God and will have no other gods before Him
(most of us are jealous people and do not know how to
handle anyone other than ourselves loving the person we
love). But we understand that about God in the sense of wor-

ship and profession of faith. We do not see it, or at least respect it, in the same way when it comes to sex.

God's promise is to His people, those who are called by His name, just as a husband's vow is to his wife, not any other woman. If God gave everyone, including the people who denied him, the same benefits as those of us who have accepted him and have lived with the persecution for naming His name, why would we serve Him? Earthly perspective: Why as a woman would I preserve myself for a man who has freely given *my* gift to any woman who asked for it? In the same sense, why would we choose to present ourselves to our earthly husband as one "called by his name" when we've allowed others to call us by theirs? If we honor, value, and respect him for his position in our lives, we would want to present ourselves pure.

The problem lies in the waiting. We do not know who we are going to marry or if we will even get married. We take ourselves out of the game by choosing to tell God, "I am okay if I miss whatever blessing you had in store for me; you've been good enough." We do not trust God with our future because what we see right now is all our minds can handle. We fall so deeply in "love" with what we have or want, which could be sent by God, that we do not allow Him to mature us nor the blessing for His ultimate purpose.

The beautiful thing about God is even though most of us fit into the category of "taking life into my own hands" God has still cleansed us, blessed us, shown his grace and mercy to us. We must, therefore, be careful not to shame people for their missteps when God has forgiven us of ours. The Bible says there is no condemnation for those who are in Christ Jesus (Romans 8:1). What this means is, once someone has confessed and repented, God does not hold them to condemnation. Yet that is what most people feel and receive, especially from other Christians. If we are modeling our lives after Christ, our response should always be love as evidenced through correction and compassion. When the Pharisees brought the woman caught in adultery to Jesus to be stoned, He extended mercy and compassion, and told her to sin no more (John 8:1-11). He did not shame her. He did not look down upon her. He showed her His love.

Sometimes we develop the attitude of, "they know better than to come over here with that mess." As a part of our culture and even how we practice our faith, obvious sins of others become a pathway for us to place ourselves higher than we ought to. Because we teach virginity, and hardly ever anything beyond that, we indirectly teach "this is not the place to be if you've had sex." We do not talk about. We do not help people through it. We support bills that close down Planned Parenthoods but we allow sexual assaulters free from lack of sufficient evidence. We teach that the Bible is "pro-life" yet with a lack of convictions, we tell women that their bodies only function in response to what a man wants from it, and therefore her life only matters as much as the man she's involved with, voluntarily or involuntarily, deems it so. Sex becomes taboo and people look to the world for love and acceptance. But the world will only tell them what they want to hear and not lead them back into the place where God would have them to be. The least we could do is encourage those coming after us to seek Him first and allow Him to add those things which are desired (Matthew 6:33). Obedience is always better than sacrifice.

I pray for the young girls and boys coming up in today's time. Sexual perversion is beginning earlier and earlier and the innocence of our children is being stripped away before they are old enough to understand what has happened. Whether by choice, influence, or falling victim to underage sex trafficking, our children are growing up without a chance to make the decisions we treated as liberating. To those of you who have chosen chastity as a way of life until God sends you your mate, I pray you always view your decision as one in obedience and reverence to God, to bring glory and honor to His name. If you aren't sure why you've made that choice, I pray God reveals your intentions because it is with the heart that God deals with people.

And it is in our hearts that we know our truths.

I once had a mentor with whom I never felt comfortable enough sharing that I was not a virgin. We were so much alike and had developed a sisterly love for each other that was encouraging and refreshing, though it lasted only a short while. Herself a Christian, as well, and a few years older than I, she managed to remain a virgin even throughout a long relationship. For that I admired her, maybe a little more than I should have. I'd never heard her use profanity, she always talked about Jesus in her life, and she extended love towards me simply because of who I was—or maybe, once she was convinced of who I really was. As life would have it, personal decisions made by each of us would place a strain on the relationship we had begun to develop. Over the course of years and several attempts to reconcile, I saw a side of her that I would have never expected to see. I could hardly convince myself that this was in fact the same person. But at that point in my life, I was able to recognize the broken parts of her because I shared those same broken parts. Though in my heart I wish what has become of us did not have to be, seeing her brokenness showed me how much more I needed to grow.

When you meet people, who remind you so much of yourself, you cannot ignore the ugly parts of them. You take the good and the bad and you learn from it. I learned that you could do everything the "right" way, be notorious for you work ethic, stand as an example for which others chose to follow, present your life a pure Christian, but with a broken, unattended heart, all of that falls to pieces. As I listened to her broken heart break mine, I thought about the hearts I had broken. I thought about all the people I allowed to be used as collateral damage as I "climbed my way to the top." For years I had been stuck on what happened to me, but there were other people involved, who by no fault of their own, got caught in the cross fire and I never attended to their hearts after I'd been the reason for their pain.

Perfectionism will keep you from being honest with yourself. It will convince you of lies and half-truths to protect your image to yourself. Other people will have their opinions, but as long as you still see yourself as faultless and the victim, you can go to sleep easily at night. Perfection will remind you of all the ways you've been done wrong and erase the ways in which you've done wrong. It will tell you that you had a right to behave the way you did, to say the things you said. It hinders you from asking for forgiveness and it hinders you from extending forgiveness. Perfectionist are self-centered, yet outwardly focused. As each issue within yourself manifests, you find an issue in someone else to focus on. It is crippling to your personal growth and maturity and it is hurtful to the people around you. Especially if the person you need to forgive moves on and finds joy and peace, you will stay bitter and forever remind them of "that time when."

Perfection was the disease of the Pharisees and some early Jewish-Christian converts. Knowledgeable of the law, the erudite of their day, they failed to recognize Jesus as the one who fulfilled the law and He was right in front of their faces. Jesus gave them freedom and they chose bondage. Jesus still extends freedom and we choose bondage. The church has taught bondage by way of shame and condemnation. False doctrines teach bondage or lead us into bondage by justifying our sins and allowing us to stay comfortable in them. Jesus says He is the way, the truth, and the life (John 14:6). By no other way can anyone get to God, yet it is by all those other ways that we attempt to reach Him. It is not by how much right or wrong we do, it is about whether or not we allow God to take control of our lives and we live them in submission to His will for us.

We can easily fall into the role of the early Jews who had begun to believe in Jesus as the Messiah, but then went back to the law. Think about it. The man who they all believed to be their Savior died, and though that's not how the story ended, they reverted back to what they knew before Jesus entered their lives. Sometimes what we know (logic and reason) hinders us from exercising faith. And it doesn't have to come in the form of a degree or accolade, though most times it will. Sometimes we've been through too much to rely on faith. Sometimes, it is not always what we want to know and believe, but that which we have no other choice to.

Consider the mothers of the victims of police brutality here in the United States of America. I cannot imagine being in their shoes and having to hear someone tell me, "just have faith." In what? This justice system that continues to prove that our pain does not matter and our children are dispensable? That surely will not bring their children back. Too often in Christian circles have we developed the attitude that we are not supposed to *feel*. Because we *know* that God is good, and He is, we do not allow people the time and space to appropriately deal with their feelings. We have taught that the Lord will handle whatever the situation, and He will. But what do we do in the mean time? From the time the hurt begins to the time we are *supposed* to heal, how do we manage that time of unanswered questions and unattended emotions? The Bible tells us that there is a time for everything, including a time to mourn, grieve, weep, and heal (Ecclesiastes 3:1-9). If we continue to teach people to move on from that which dramatically impacts their lives, we will continue to have a people who are always grieving, always mourning, always weeping, and never healed. We must create safe spaces where people are allowed the opportunity to express their human emotions so that they can make room to move from where they are to a healthier, whole place. No one is the same after a loss. Combine loss with no assurance of justice, and nowhere to turn to after a "not guilty" verdict, you will have a people with no faith, no trust, fueled by grief and anger, continually in pain.

Before I became pregnant with my first son, I had a recurring dream of me running through a dark, empty valley, holding a baby boy with bullets flying past me. We never got hit, but I never stopped running, either. The first time I heard the words "it is a boy!", one million and five emotions ran through my body. Would I be able to raise him? Protect him? Because he's Black he will always be a target and because he's male, he will always be assumed to be the aggressor. There is a powerlessness that rests upon the shoulders of every woman given the responsibility to raise a black male child. With or without the presence or help of their fathers, to know you are raising your son in a world that will kill him simply for being born is the reality we face day in and day out. There is no option to have faith in the justice system; it fails our sons, just as it failed Jesus.

I think about Mary. How her first-born son was brutally crucified in front of her face, hanging from a tree. His body beaten bloody and his face unrecognizable. The judge of his day found no fault. They could not find a crime to pin on him. There was no evidence against him. He did not talk back. He did not resist. He did not show any signs of apparent threat, yet they beat him to death, in front of his mother.

I pray the Lord's protection over my sons daily. Though one is a toddler and the other not yet born, the evil systems of this world are set up against them, and all I can do is plead the blood of Jesus over their lives, now. I pray for the mothers who have lost their sons to a faulty justice system. I pray that the comfort that Jesus had to send for his own mother reaches into their hearts and homes and provides them with enough strength to keep going, keep fighting, and know that despite the outlook of her circumstances, God knows her exact pain and will not leave her side. I pray that even after the worst form of attack, each mother stands tall and speaks life about her son, even if the world has denied him his very breath.

It is not only in highly religious circles, or the exact opposite, that the enemy wants to keep our minds off of God. In fact, it is in the everyday realities with which we struggle he hits us the hardest. It would make sense for a mother to give up after being hit with something like this. But it would make the devil mad when she chooses not to. Grief, mourning, and even questioning God is normal. God does not expect us to be as robots, void of feeling and emotion. He understands our hearts and our pain—because even He had to turn his face from looking upon all the sin Jesus carried on the cross.

We will get weak. We will struggle. We will face hard times and tragedy, and not simply because we are Christians (though that will sometimes be the cause), but because we are living. Christian circles for too long have taught that believers can never experience doubt, depression, heart ache. We are expected to always smile and admit to false happiness. Though our joy is in the Lord, He knows that some days will not be as easy, but He has given us His grace to carry us through the hard and dark times.

In 2 Corinthians 12, Paul tells us about his thorn, an affliction he calls a messenger of Satan. Though he is never specific about what that thorn is, we know it is something that he prayed God would remove from his life. After going to God three times, Paul tells us that the Lord told him, "My grace is sufficient for you, for my power is made perfect in your weakness (2 Corinthians 12:9)." Paul continues to say, "Therefore I will boast all the more gladly about my weaknesses, so that Christ's power may rest on me. That is why, for Christs sake, I delight in weaknesses, in insults, in hardships, in persecution, in difficulties. For when I am weak, then I am strong (12:9-10)."

We do not have to pretend that things are always good. In fact, when we share what God is doing and has done in our lives, He uses those very things to empower us. We have been taught to keep our mouths shut and keep people out of our business—and we do need to practice discretion; your testimony doesn't have to include every detail of your life—but we should never keep our mouths shut about what God has done in our lives. You never know how your story may touch someone else and give them just what they needed to keep believing and keep trusting.

God will not remove every pain, every hardship, every difficulty, every weakness, but He will give you His power to continue to live through it. He will help you to grow through it. He will use everything done to you and against you for His glory and for your good. He will use every hardship you face and give you His strength to overcome. Romans 8:28 tells us, "and we know that in *all* things God works for the good of those who love him, who have been called according to his purpose (emphasis mine)." That means even those things that we think are unspeakable—and we all have unspeakable secrets—God will turn it around to work for your good.

Because we know this, we do not have to carry the weight of keeping everything together all the time. We do not have to beat up on ourselves every time we miss the mark. We do not have to try to please everyone. We do not have to worry about what has been said about us. We do not have to try to handle and fix everything. We can let it go. We can live in the freedom, the grace, and the power of the Holy Spirit.

We practice perfection when we are truly searching for wholeness. Emptiness and voids cause us to fill our lives with more *stuff*. Whether its worry, guilt, shame, judgement of others, busyness laziness, people, excuses, fears, jealousies, work, school—we all have something that we add to our lives to make us full, yet we still feel empty. Jesus is asking that we choose Him. Better than any drug, any drink, and overexertion of misplaced energy, He is the only person who can fill the empty places and make us whole.

If you are struggling with feelings of inadequacies no matter how hard you try, if you feel like every day you give your all and still it is not good enough, I invite you to have a talk with Jesus. He's always available, always listening, and always ready to change your life. Do not worry about not knowing how to pray—prayer is simply a conversation between you and God. You do not need long seminarian and theological words. You need an open heart with space for him to come in. Cast your burdens on Him and may you experience the peace that surpasses your understanding.

If you need help getting started, use this prayer and make it personal for your needs.

"Dear God,

Thank you for speaking to my heart. Thank you for showing me the areas in which I need to surrender to you. Thank you for not condemning me, but for loving me to yourself. Forgive me for making little gods out of the mundane and losing my focus of you. Lord, I need you to step into my life and fill the empty places. I've been hurting. I've been down. I am exhausted. I need new life. I need a fresh encounter with you. I need the worst to be behind me. I need you to lift my spirit, lift my head, lift me, Lord! Move me and mold me into a whole and healthy person. Help me to live my life as a testimony of you grace, your love, your power. May my testimony draw more hearts to You.

In Jesus' name I pray,
Amen."

The Pain
of Perfection

*"You are confined
by your own system of oppression."*
— Toni Morrison

rowing up I had an idea of who I wanted to be—a wife, a mother, a successful career woman, a home maker, a friend everyone could count on. Pretty much, I wanted to be Claire Huxtable. She was beautiful, intelligent, independent, adored by her husband and respected by her children. If there ever was a total package, she was it. I spent my life trying to become just like Claire Huxtable, being the total package as designed for me. But somewhere along the way, I had to accept that Claire Huxtable was a fictional character and while there may be someone out there who is the real-life version, honey…it ain't me.

Here's why:

1. My body was not built like that before children, nor after 1. So, after 5?? Give me a break, already.
2. The whole lawyer thing…yeah, Business Law killed that dream.
3. The just-as-successful, supportive, doting husband who can be home from work when you cannot, whom never gets mad (fiction, again).
4. Most importantly, it is just not my path.

Both Claire and Heathcliff came from emotionally, financially, and apparently mentally stable, though quite goofy, two-parent households. Before they even began with their own family, they had a pretty good idea of how the whole family thing was supposed to work. Both were highly educated with well-paying careers, not just jobs, and had enough down time to spend with their family to develop healthy relationships. They represented the goal for most families, but hardly the reality. Even without coming from such a background, though, we all have something to be proud of, on which we can build a strong family unit. It may not look like the Huxtables, but it will look like God's hand touched it, fixed it, blessed it, and favored it if we trust that God is working everything out for our good (Romans 8:28).

Of my favorite child hood memories are the trips my family would take to Alabama to visit my mother's side. There was never much to do besides fishing, eating, fishing again, and eating a whole lot more. But those summers meant everything to me. Being with my cousins, staying up all night eating Blue Bell ice cream, sweet potato pie, coconut pie, chocolate cake, red velvet cake, sock-it-to-me cake, and waking up to the aromas of fried green tomatoes and Conecuh County Sausage—I was able to develop bonds with my cousins who lived thousands of miles away that still hold the same weight to this day. Beyond eating good, getting a few shades darker and developing a southern twang in my vocabulary, I loved going to Alabama because it always felt like whatever "home" was supposed to feel like. Mama'nem called it home because that's what is was for them. I called it home because that's what it felt to me.

My great granddaddy only had a fourth-grade education, but he farmed the land he owned, raised 10 of his very own children and a number of their children, and their children's children. I didn't have much time to be with him but the memory of his voice, his smile, and the legacy he left through each of his children and their children always made Evergreen, Alabama home to me. In Evergreen, there is no hustle and bustle to keep up with. The Joneses are probably your cousins and therefore there is no need to keep up with them, either. As a child, what Alabama gave me was a sense of belonging. My light skin and long hair was never an issue with my family like it was for folks in Los Angeles. I was their blood and my family always treated me as such.

As an adult I realized, that just as I have complaints about Los Angeles, some relatives had complaints about

Alabama. The rich history of the segregated south was never apparent to me when I visited, though my family lived through and experienced some of the worst of those times. Beyond that, the family that I visited was just my mother's maternal side, though her paternal side lived in the very same town.

My maternal grandfather died the year I was born. He and my mother didn't have a relationship and he wasn't spoken of much at all. In fact, the first time I heard his name was when my dad said that my mom said, "You are just like OJ (OJ is not his name, but out of respect for his living family, we will call him such)." I did not know who OJ was nor what being just like him meant. Evidently it made my dad upset, so I inferred OJ must not have been that great of a person. It was not until I was much older and writing fiction that this person, OJ, this unknown character in my life, began to matter to me. What was he like? What did he look like? I saw a picture of OJ's mom once and saw myself. Her hair, long and thick like mine. Her broad build, her yellow skin. Here I was looking at someone with whom I shared much resemblance, but would never know anything about. I began to develop the disdain towards OJ that my mother never showed. She had her granddaddy and he was all the father she said she needed. But I became mad for her, and when I began to replay the first time I heard his name, I was even more angry. They say little girls look for their dads in the men that they choose. Daddy said mama said he was just like hers, but she didn't even know him? How was that fair?

One of the worst side effects of perfection is the inability to forgive. When people hurt a perfectionist, you can almost always expect that relationship to end. We do not know how to recover from broken foundations and thus we choose to move on to the next. One of the beauties of being made whole in Christ, however, is the acquiring the ability to be honest about pain and learning to forgive others for how their actions either directly or indirectly affected you.

I was about 8 or 9 years old when my mom told my sisters and me to pack our things. For that age, I had no business being excited that my parents were splitting up. But I knew I was going to stay with my best-friend/cousin and that was enough to put some urgency into my packing. That wasn't completely it, though. Early on I developed "daddy issues" that I would always be aware of but never really deal with. I never wanted to hurt my dad by telling him "I have this issue with you," or "it really hurt me when you said this." So, most times I said nothing. I learned to bottle in my emotions and wait until I was with my mom to release them. She almost always said something to him for me, which almost always led to a fight, which made me stop talking. Eventually I would begin writing poetry in attempts to make sense of the thoughts I had in my head concerning my life and what it had become/was becoming. Yet even with not knowing how to healthily deal with my feelings, I always loved my dad and would still be excited to see him, hear from him, and do things with him. But he was the only person that could hurt me, and after each disappointment, I grew numb to feeling or expecting anything from him. I even developed this picture of a perfect father, husband, and family that I knew I would one day have and I convinced myself it would never look anything like that of the family I was born into.

It is not like I never wanted my parents to work out. At a point in time I sincerely thought I could help them mend their broken marriage. I found a letter my mom began writing to my dad in her bedroom. I say hers because my dad slept on the couch for most of the time I remember while my parents were still together. I took the letter to the living room to read it and I left it there, right by the couch. I do not remember why I left our apartment that day, but when I got back, my dad had responded to the letter. What did I do? I read it first to make sure he said something nice, then I took it to the bedroom. I played messenger only a few more times before my dad began sleeping in the bedroom again. Not that they were alone, my sisters refused to give up their space in the big bed. I slept in the room that was supposed to be for me and my sisters and a huge part of my little mind felt like I fixed it all.

But I was a child, and the magnitude of the issues my parents had were not going to be fixed with a few letters and my parents sleeping in the same bed. Daddy was back on the couch soon after and the fighting ensued. Then I felt responsible for making them, and all of us, feel like there was a little hope.

My mom never spoke badly of my dad to me. Even when I would cry to her about how he hurt my feelings or just share my frustrations with the way he chose to handle certain issues concerning me and my sisters, she would tell me everything was going to be okay. As much as she never spoke badly of him, she didn't have much to say highly of him, either. And it is in that silence that I had room to fill in the blanks for myself. Every time a woman called our landline, or Daddy reeked of alcohol, I understood my mom's silence. I grew skeptical of any woman I was ever introduced to while alone with my dad and clung to my mom more than ever. Memories that I'd hoped would be of just me and my dad were tainted with the sounds of annoying, flirtatious laughter that brought me to tears every time I looked at my mom. I could not understand what was so wrong but I began to want freedom for her without even knowing it was happening.

As we were packing to go stay with my grandma for what was supposed to be 2 weeks, the most vivid childhood memory I have to date replayed over and over in my head and I packed faster and faster.

My mom was on the phone while she and I were folding clothes. My dad burst into the room, already frustrated about something. The details of the argument are too far past and distant to recall, but the experience can never be erased. The argument moved from the bedroom to the dining room. As each parent stood on either side of our dining room table, which had become a piece for decoration more than anything, and the screaming went from one person to another, soon that dining room table was in the air. With one hand, my dad lifted the wooden six seater dining room table and flung it against the wall. I remember my mom covering her face for protection and my sisters and I screaming, begging, pleading for him to calm down. He came toward us and slammed the hallway door shut so tightly, the three of us could not open it. As we pushed with all of the might three small children could muster, my mom opened the door. We ran to her, crying. She held us.

I cannot be sure who called him, but our pastor at the time arrived shortly after. While he was trying to get my parents to talk through what had happened, I heard brokenness in each of their voices. I heard people who once loved each other fighting to express feelings that would contradict those that brought them together in the first place. Then daddy was gone. The police had arrived. And life from that point on would always be different. My views of family, marriage, and fatherhood had all been defined at that very moment. But not the way you might think. Watching my parents fall apart, literally, made me desire a whole family more than ever before. But I knew little to nothing about that type of love, and my first attempt was more than an epic fail.

I am still not sure what dating at 14 is supposed to look like. In hindsight, I am sure of what it was not supposed to be. In graduate school, I had an assignment to write a letter to my future daughter in which I had to share wisdom I would want her to know. Here is how my points of wisdom began:

1. Your high school boyfriend does not love you.

Though I know there are a few exceptions to this rule—as I know people who met in middle school and are still happily married to this day—the truth, for the most of us, is simply that. High school is not the place where, or better yet, the *time* in which you will begin cultivating an everlasting, unconditional, fighting through thick and thin love. Most people do not yet even know what they want to be in high school. Even further, most people have not yet changed their minds about what they want to be and are still figuring it out. For those who are able to do so, that is a special and rare type of love that should be celebrated. I believe that generations past were more capable of achieving love at such an early age, but times have changed and so have we as people. For most of us, high school love is a learning experience from which we should grow. That doesn't make that boy, or you, a bad person. It is simply a reality. Even as adults, we are constantly changing and trying to find out who we are, what we like, what we want to do. Knowing that of yourself and committing to stay with something through that at such an early age is simply rare.

My high school girl friends and I experienced some of the most ridiculous things with our boyfriends. We all hated each other's boyfriends, but we still stayed with them or started dating someone else who was no better. I stuck with one, for the most part. We "broke up" so many times I would not be able to keep count. But I know that I did because I did not want my first attempt at love to be seen as a failure. I know that I wanted us to "make it" to prove to myself and everyone else, "see, I can still have a real love." But every woman has a breaking point, and my prayer for the upcoming generation is that you never have to reach it because of a puppy-love romance that went too long.

I vowed myself and God a year without being anyone's girlfriend. I wanted to talk to different guys. See what I liked and did not like. As each one of those attempts failed, and rather quickly, I had to figure out how I allowed myself to become so lost in one person that even I could not recognize who I had become. The answer did not come as quickly as I had hoped. In fact, only in recent years has it become clear—I never knew how to love a man properly.

The complexity of my relationship with my father spilled over into every attempt at a relationship with another man. I could like a guy for the fun and excitement of him, but how did I deal with the things that were not fun, exciting, romantic, respectful? Remember when I said I listened to a boy tell me how to incorrectly spell "totally"? Yeah, I had a crush on him even after he made me embarrass myself—and I did not even need him to tell me how to spell "totally"!

How did I deal with making choices for a guy that I did not necessarily want but knew would make him happy? How did I "forgive" so easily that which should have made me run away and never return? Because I only knew numbness to that which hurt me. I never allowed myself to feel the pain. I never allowed myself to wallow in it. Sure, I cried. Ate a bunch of ice cream and had nights with my girls that consisted of us trying to make each other feel better. But that was it.

Because I could never face my dad, the first man I loved, I could never face any other man I would consider a "love" either. I hid my feelings, dealt with things privately, and tried to be a version of me that they could accept. This meant that, at times, I was completely checked out of who I knew I was. Patterns and behaviors that were completely contradictory to my character became my norm. Not because I wanted them to, either. But because for them, I wanted to be the perfect girl.

While it is true that little boys need their fathers, it is equally as true for little girls. Some of us, like me, grow up with fathers with whom our relationships are quite complex. I knew my dad loved me, but I never felt good enough for him. It didn't matter how many times he would tell me that was not true, his actions dictated my feelings and I could only go off of how I felt. He was not completely absent from my upbringing nor was he completely present, and that in and of itself creates a peculiar dynamic. Others of us, like my mom, never really knew our fathers, except that they fit the description of the Temptations' hit song, *Papa Was a Rolling Stone*. What we know of fatherhood comes from other men—uncles, grandfathers, cousins, brothers—who have stepped in and tried to fill their shoes. But even still, there is a longing, if for nothing else, for identity. Most girls simply want to know, "why didn't daddy love me? Why wasn't I enough?" That tiny seed of doubt grows into a whirlwind of problems.

I was fortunate enough, and truly blessed, to find an earthly love who made it easy for me to let go of those feelings of insecurities. At least long enough for me to say yes and meet him at the end of the aisle. But being married revealed that I still had to deal with the feelings even if they weren't as present anymore. The only way to do that was to fall in love with Jesus and rest safely in His arms.

Over and over, scripture tells us how much God loves us. He tells us that before he even formed us in our mother's womb, He knew us (Jeremiah 1:5). He tells us that we are fearfully and wonderfully made (Psalm 139:14). He tells us that even when our earthly parents abandon us, He will never forsake us (Psalm 27:10). He tells us that He has a purpose and a plan for our lives (Jeremiah 29:11). God constantly shows us that His love is one that cannot be beat. It cannot be matched. But it can be imitated. As I learned about the character of God, how He sees me through His eyes, I learned that I have to love me in the same way. I have to believe about me that things that God believes about me or else I am saying that He is a liar. I would love to tell you that this is as easy as ABC and 123, like the Jackson 5 claimed. But it is not. It takes time and deliberate and intentional addressing of all the negative things we believed about ourselves and why.

To understand my dad, I had to learn about what made him the way he was. By doing so, I learned that it is not only women who can have daddy issues. If we want to get really real, there are probably as many men with daddy issues as there are women (this is just an observation—not backed by any scientific study). Because if you examine the men you know and how many of them were raised by their fathers, respect their fathers, admire and reverence their fathers, want to be their fathers, you may find that number to be very small. The father, the head of the household from God's perspective, holds so much weight, that until a man decides that he will not become his father, with the help of God and God alone, does the cycle begin to break. My father had two fathers — his biological and a step-father, both of whom his relationships were not simple. The streets taught him how to be a man. He did the best he could with what he knew and that which he never wanted to be, he did his best to never become. Sometimes our desire to not be like that which we experienced is so strong, it is exactly what we become.

I had already realized that I learned to ignore things done by men I loved and excuse them without addressing how they affected me. I learned that, like my mother, I didn't have to speak badly about a person, but I sure would not speak highly of them either. Silence. Though a technique that passed time, hardly an effective coping mechanism and even worse healing strategy. When you seek personal wellness and wholeness without blaming others for how you feel, though, God will give you His heart and teach you how to love like Him. That does not mean that you will magically have fairytale relationships. But you will learn forgiveness, and compassion, and you will be able to move on without expecting anything from anyone first.

I thought September 7, 2013 would be the most emotional day of my life. It was the day I had always dreamed of and the person I was marrying was more than I could have ever dreamed of. For that reason alone, I just knew I would be a crying mess. But as I stood in the reception hall, waiting for the bridal party to finish making their way down the aisle, I had my arm wrapped around my dad's. The time was coming for me to marry the love of my life and my daddy was going to lead me to him. Except, he was shaking more than me, and chewing on his gum like a nervous cow and all the picture evidence proves this (thanks, Dad). I asked him, "You alright? You're supposed to be holding me up. Don't let me fall walking down this aisle." He laughed, "Yeah, I'm good, kid." We made it down the aisle and he released me to my husband. Our ceremony was performed and I made it through without one single tear. For people who really know me, that was the true accomplishment of the day. In all seriousness, I was able to look at my husband and trust that the vow I was making to him would not be made in vain. Joy filled my heart and you could not erase my smile if you tried.

The time came in the reception for the daddy-daughter dance. I had decided that I would split my song in half because as much as it meant to my dad to give away his daughter, I knew what that meant for my mother, as well. I chose *My Wish* by Rascal Flats as our song because not only did I know it is what my dad really wanted for me, even if he never really knew how to express it, it was truly what I wanted for him. From broken-ness, he tried with all his humanly might—and my dad is a strong man—to be a better man and father than what he had experienced. He loved the best he knew how, and though he fell a few times, he never stayed down. He fought his way towards wellness and being the best version of himself, and for that I will always be proud of him. As the song began to play, it didn't take long before my dad's face was filled with tears and his head was resting on my shoulder.

"Daddy, I sent you the song before-hand so you could listen to it." He hadn't and that was clear, though also expected.

He responded, "Yeah, but I didn't know it was a country western. Where's your mom?"

What was supposed to be a minute with my dad was much shorter as his emotions got the best of him, but it was more than enough. I kissed him on his cheek and he and my mom switched places. He walked away, trying to shake the tears and redness from his face and I finished my dance with the most amazing mother I could have ever asked for. Just as quickly as tears filled my dad's face, tears had filled mine as my mom and I embraced. Every time I have watched my wedding video, that segment always reminds me that even from a mess of brokenness, God can still restore. I had always desired to be that little girl who could cry to daddy, but what God allowed was for my daddy to cry on me. And He gave me a mother strong enough to handle all of those tears.

The next year for my birthday my dad gave me a card in which he told me I was his hero. I broke down the same way he had at my wedding. We had a lot of missed dates, misunderstandings, and disagreements. But the fact remains, God gave him to me and me to him, and even with a complicated beginning, God has the final say so.

Being able to love my dad for who he is and not who I wanted him to be took time. I first had to accept that I was holding things against him that God had already forgiven him for. Marriage taught me that. I mentioned earlier in this chapter the lack of effective communication I witnessed from my parents. Well, we emulate what we see. Not only did I not really know how to communicate my feelings properly, I did not really know how to live with a man. For most of my upbringing, it was just girls, girls, girls. We didn't have to even think about men and anything they may like or prefer. We knew our dads, but we didn't live with them, and when we all came home, it was just us girls. Marriage showed me all the ways in which I needed to let God really lead my life. Not because I was trying so hard to lead myself—though that was a part of it, too—but mainly because I truly had no idea what I was doing.

If marriage is anything, its selfless. The healthiest marriages are made of two people who understand that concept. It is constant growth and forgiveness, and the will to push forward.

I had never seen that done. Not properly. I remember in marriage counseling I was asked, "what do you think the purpose of marriage is?" I responded, "to be a representation on earth of Christ' love for his church." I did believe that. I do believe that. But I did not understand that.

What does that actually look like? When we think of the way Christ loves us, do we really acknowledge all the times we break His heart? All the times we break our promises? All the times we fall short of His expectations? All the times we place other people or things before Him? And each time, He loves us back to Himself.

If you never want to be disappointed, if you want to keep the idea of a perfect man intact, if you want to continue to think of yourself as perfect, do not get married. Everyone who has witnessed a wedding has heard the words, "marriage is something you do not enter into lightly", and they say that because sometimes it gets heavy.

The picture of marriage, and even that portrayed by married people, shows happiness and fullness, which does come if both people are truly committed to God, each other, and their vows. I find no greater joy than the days I can just be with my husband and son without being pulled away by anything else—outside obligations, work, other family members, cleaning, cooking. Those moments that hold no monetary value and can never be replaced. We now have several mediums to try and capture those moments instantly, and sometimes we share them through social media. But I will say that the best moments of life cannot be shared. If we get stuck in trying to capture everything, we will miss the moments, and those are truly irreplaceable.

So yes, there is blessing that comes with the unity of marriage and having your own family. But even behind all the Instagram shots of the ring and proposal, cake tasting and dress picking, wedding and reception, home and children, matching clothes and shoes, there are real people working every day to keep those smiles. Life does not stop to happen once the vows are shared and the broom has been jumped. In fact, because a decision to honor God has been made, attacks begin to come from directions you never knew existed. That does not mean those people are not happy, but social media shows highlight reels for a reason—every day is not sunshine and rainbows. Even if they were, once you develop a perfect persona, people are not quick to forgive once you fail. Social media is also not the place to be real. If married people were completely honest all the time on social media, they would be criticized for "putting their business out there" and quite frankly, people would stop caring. It is the fantasy of perfection which draws the attention of those who desire it.

That does not mean, however, that all happy marriages are actually ones to be skeptical about. We see stories on the news about people "who seemed so happy" end in a tragedy and then everyone becomes skeptical of the happily married couple. They start speculating and gossiping, "well, I heard he made her do this," and, "well, she said he would not do that." Transgressions of people's past become the focus instead of where the couple is headed. When the news reports that "no one would have ever saw this coming," they are really inferring, "they seemed so perfect." And there it is again, this idea that nothing can go wrong.

I had the dream of a perfect marriage. It did not take too many first arguments before doubt started to creep into my mind. "We never argued like this before. What did he really mean by that? Maybe I am keeping him from being all he really wants to be? Maybe we were too young? What in Jesus' name am I really doing? I did not sign up for this!" The minute my idea of perfection was tainted, Satan went full force. Just as God knows your dreams and plans, so does Satan. He will even use something admirable like wanting a marriage that pleases God and turn it into something to bring you guilt and shame. More than spending every day with my husband, and living through life's up and downs with him by my side, my desire for a perfect marriage became a god. I only realized this after feeling like my whole world had ended because of a rough patch my husband and I experienced.

Why would my world be over? God had done so much for me, why would I think that because we weren't talking that everything I had ever worked for was in vain? I began this chapter referencing the Huxtables and their "perfect image", and acknowledging that God doesn't need us to be the Huxtables to bless our marriages and our families. I had to really let that sink in. As much as I never heard my mother speak lowly of my father, I never heard my grandmother speak lowly of OJ, either. She raised six kids, while in nursing school (and eventually becoming a nurse), had seventeen grandkids and the number of great grandkids is slowly but surely starting to catch up. With that blood in my veins, why would I think because my husband and I weren't getting along that my *world* was ending?

Because I placed all my focus and attention on what I had instead of who gave it to me. I placed all the expectations of a perfect husband, marriage, and father onto my husband and expected him to carry them without ever disappointing me. It is his responsibility, right? As the head of the household? Doesn't the church teach us that men are strong and women are weaker? These things were his problems, not mine. Right?

I'll be the first, but hopefully not the last, to tell you that being Christian wife takes a strong woman. When we set our eyes on pleasing God and not the world—not our cultures, not our families, not our own ideas of what marriage should me—we strap on battle gear that we can never take off. I unknowingly placed all that had hurt me, all that which I did not understand, all that which I never wanted to be said of my marriage onto my husband and expected that he would handle it.

But he is not God.

The most unfair thing we can do to our spouses is expect them to provide and keep our happiness. We place a burden of responsibility on them they will never be able to achieve. Without paying any attention, we elevated them to the place where God and God alone should be. They become the center of our lives, the focus of all our attention, and unfairly, the recipient of all our pain. Equally unfair to your spouse is for you to stop being you. Trying to be everything for someone will inevitable lead you down a road to emptiness, bitterness, resentment, and loneliness. Hopefully you did not get married to change everything about yourself. Hopefully, you married someone who chose you as you were and you both decided to make your separate lives work together as one. If you have done that, you cannot lose yourself. A marriage only works when both parties are living their best lives, supporting each other.

Your spouse is not your competition. Every win or lose, you take it as a team. You do not have to pretend to be perfect, but you keep people who would judge you for not being perfect away from your union. Like I said before, I had never seen a successful marriage. As I felt the image of my marriage was becoming less of what I wanted it to be, I thought of all the ways people would judge me as a wife for not having that to turn back to. I made up in my mind all the negative things people could say about me and my family when it came to men and marriage. I thought about how I could easily fall into the cyclical pattern of broken homes. But when you seek after God, and you give Him your heart, He will not only free your mind from negative thinking, but send you people to reassure you that you are not alone and you cannot worry about what other people think. Your spouse is your spouse. Your marriage is your marriage. Unless others are praying for you, edifying you, and taking you before the feet of Jesus, you do not allow them around the sanctity of your marriage.

I was not failing and was most certainly not a failure. I had faith that my union was blessed by God, but I had to accept that I had not been the best steward over my blessings. God showed me all the ways and times I had pushed him over to make room for the way I thought I had to fix things. He revealed to me all the times He gave me instructions and I passed on his plan. He convicted me of the times when I prayed for His hand to move then I forgot about Him once He delivered. Then finally, after reaching complete exhaustion, I prayed, "Lord, it is yours. You gave it to me, and I am tired of trying to be you. Fix it." That prayer has since grown into more detail and God continues to show me just how much He has left to do in me.

See, when you live with perfectionism all your life, your first reaction is to identify the problem, search for the solution, take the attention off of yourself, and then take credit for the resolution.

That is not what God desires of us. Trying to fix everything and hold everything together that you clearly need to surrender will take you to places that are so far out of your character, you will not recognize yourself. You will wish you can erase the memory and you will start over compensating to make up for your lapse in character. You lose control, in the negative sense, and you may even display behaviors that completely contradict who you are and all that God has created you to be. This is certainly a ploy of the enemy, to prove to God that we are not as faithful to Him as we claim.

But God has offered us a way out. He has told us that he will fight our battles if we just be still (Exodus 14:14). He has prepared us by telling us just how the enemy will attack and showing us how to guard ourselves against them (Ephesians 6). Holding on to the idea of perfection will cause you to let go of God's hand. You will need every ounce of strength you have to try to handle that which was never intended for you to handle, especially by yourself. You will grow tired, you will get weary, you will need a life line to pull you back up to safety.

The blessing is in knowing that *you* let go, not God. He's still right there, and He's still waiting for you. Take hold of His hand. Let the strength you have been trying to carry on your own be renewed by His almighty power.

I had to learn the true meaning of love in order to love and feel loved. I pray that wherever you are in life—single, married, divorced—you know how much God loves you and no matter what the world tells you should become of you, be confident of this: "He who began a good work in you will carry it on to completion until the day of Christ Jesus (Philippians 1:6)."

God is not done with you. Keep going.

4

The **Price**
of Perfection

> "I'm gonna make a gospel record
> and tell Jesus that I cannot bear
> these burdens alone."
> — Aretha Franklin

_J_ can never thank my mom enough for her diligence in raising my sisters and me in church. In my adult life, I encourage myself by singing the songs of the days when choirs wore robes and marched in the sanctuary, holding up candles, symbolizing that we are to be the light of the world. I remember getting juice boxes in children's church after reciting memory verses. And Vacation Bible School—well, to be completely honest, I had to grow to love that. I once thought that when the school year ended, so did church. Summer meant freedom! But eventually, I grew to become excited about Vacation Bible School and the lessons I learned would stay with me forever. There was one lesson

I could never really get with, though. And it seemed to be one that was taught more than the others. I'll provide the scripture reference shortly, but here is the paraphrase of how I always understood this passage.

There was a dad who had two sons. One was responsible. He did his chores, never complained, made life easy for his father. The other son was lazy, self-seeking and wasteful. He was conceited, arrogant, and lacked respect and self-control. Before he was due his inheritance, he asked for it so he could go live his life the way he wanted. This is where my confusion always began—the dad gave it to him. The story goes on to say that it wasn't very many days after he received the money that it was gone. He wasted it on living like a wild child. But as soon as the money was gone, the country in which he was now residing experienced a famine, and he was in need. He had gotten so low that he was eating with the pigs. Suddenly, he comes to his senses and realizes that even his father's servants live better than that. He goes home to ask for forgiveness and asks to be a servant. But the dad throws him a party, and not just cake and ice cream for the immediate family—a huge, lavish party.

Meanwhile the other brother is still doing everything he is supposed to do, in the field—still working. The older brother was mad and refused to go to the party. Then the dad comes out to ask him why he was angry. The older brother tells him he doesn't understand—all these years he has done everything he was supposed to do and he never received such a party, but his brother, who has wasted away his inheritance and lived his life free of responsibility receives such a party. The father tells the older brother that everything that he has also belongs to him, but his younger brother was dead and lost, but now he is alive and found.

When this story was taught, the lesson was often "do not be mad like the older brother." My thought, "why not?" If a Christian life was meant for us to be obedient to God, keep his commandments, obey and honor our parents, live righteously—not riotously—what was wrong with him feeling the way he felt? Even now I still catch myself feeling like the older brother, but it took me years to see the bigger message behind this parable.

Beginning at verse 11 of Luke 15, we are introduced to a father who had two types of sons. The younger—maybe signifying not as mature or not old enough to thoroughly understand his life choices, maybe just marking the difference between the two—asks for his entire inheritance. My first thought, "what does he need with all that money? Why is he so greedy?" As I matured in my own faith walk, I was convicted. How often do I ask God—my heavenly Father—to give me this and that when I know I have not prepared myself to handle all that I am asking for. And not only do I ask for way more than I need, but I get mad if He doesn't give it to me.

Scripture goes on to say that his father gave it to him, the son left, and within a few days, it was all gone. My initial thought: he spoiled that boy. He should have been like my mama and told him to sit down somewhere. My mature thought: how many times has God given me exactly what I asked for, I failed to thank Him properly, and then I wasted away the blessing He'd given me?

Next, the son is in need. He's gotten so low that he's eating with the pigs and no man would help him. Here is when I am supposed to start feeling bad for him, right? Nope. My thought, "well, what did he expect?" He decides to go back home to his father and ask to be just a servant because he doesn't deserve to be called his son. This daddy has to be to nicest man alive. He ran to him, hugged him, kissed him and told his servants to bring him the best, of everything — clothes, food, jewelry, shoes. And they did.

Ultimate confusion. Where is the punishment? Is the Bible telling me that we can live however we want as long as we come back and apologize? Does that mean all the evil done in this world will simply be wiped away with "I'm sorry?" I could not accept that. What I could not accept even more was that teachers taught us not to be the *older* brother.

But the Holy Spirit is the master of conviction.

This lesson, this parable, is much deeper than a boy who got away with the worst type of behavior and was rewarded for it. It is much deeper than, "do not be like the older brother" as well. See the older brother—as it is taught—had a spirit of self-righteousness. He looked at all he had done and could not fathom how after all his brother had not done, his brother was rewarded. He focused on his *works*, while the condition of his *heart* was failing. The younger brother took his eyes off of what was important and chased after the world, losing all dignity and self-respect in the process. The older brother took his eyes of the purpose of his obedience and focused on his brother's disobedience. Still, this lesson is deeper than understanding each brother.

This lesson is about a father who extends his love to both in the capacity needed for each of them. He did not forget about one son when he was attending to the other. Even when the older son was angry, he took time to explain to him, love him, and meet him where he was. Which is the exact same thing he did for the younger son.

As children of God, we are all like the Prodigal Son, but many become like the older brother. If I had learned this lesson this way, maybe I would not have hated it so much growing up. But then I would not have experienced God revealing my true nature to me through His Word.

How often do we look at other people's lives and circumstances and make up in our own minds whether or not they deserve what they have? When we know too much of other people's business without knowing their testimony, we conclude that God is not fair. This parable illustrated the condition of each of the brother's hearts. When we take our eyes off serving God, as the older brother did serving his father, all we see is what someone else is doing or not doing. We miss the fact that while we have been working, while we have been diligent, while we have been responsible, while we have honored our parents, while we've never cheated, while we've never gotten in a fight, while we've never done this that or the other, God has kept us. He has provided for us. He has sustained us in and through every season of our lives *and* we have access through him to everything that He has. Instead, we envy the person who had to eat with the pigs for being loved back to redemption. We become so fixated on what was not done for us, that we miss all that was.

One of the dangers of walking with Christ casually is becoming comfortable and forgetting the little things. The older brother's worship had become routine. Maybe he lost his joy in serving. Maybe it was all out of obligation. Maybe that is why when he saw his brother had returned he was not happy for his own flesh and blood to be safe from the evil wiles of the world, yet jealous of him. How often in our lives do we become jealous of people who have endured things we could not even fathom because of how we see God move in their lives? This was the issue of the older brother. It is my prayer that if you have never had to deal with feeling like the older brother that you never have to, or you never will. But for those of us who have, redemption was not just for the younger brother. The father extends his love again to the older brother by reminding him, "you are always with me and all that I have is yours". The Bible tells us to not grow weary in well doing for in due time we will reap if we faint not (Galatians 6:9). Even when this older brother had feelings that went against what his behaviors portrayed, his father extended his love. Is that not how God loves us?

It is clear to see the way in which this parable shows God's love for the lost. Chronologically, this parable follows that of the Lost Sheep and the Lost Coin. We know that we are all lost until something happens on the inside—that change of heart, that realization that we run from God when it is He who supplies our every need in search of something the world can never give us. We are humiliated by the disgrace we experience. Humbled, we come back to God, repented, asking for his grace and mercy. Most of us get that. But many of us struggle when we get past that point and we have to live out being a Christian.

This book is titled *The Yoke of Perfection* and there are many people who believe that Christians think they are perfect, as we have previously discussed. In essence, what we claim to believe and be are followers of the only perfect man who ever lived. We strive for our lives to look like his and for others to see him through us. So, was the older brother wrong for feeling like he had done everything right and still he got nothing? While our goal is to be like Jesus, that means that we extend compassion, we give grace, we show love and mercy, especially to those in need. We are not to be so hung up on who we are and what we have and have done that we cannot meet people where they are. In fact, that's the exact opposite of who Jesus is and what He did. Jesus, who is God, perfect in all his ways, made himself into the form of a man to enter an imperfect world to save the most imperfect people. See the people who knew the law, practiced the law, obeyed the law, they forgot they were in need of Jesus. He stood before them, they saw what He had done and still denied Him. Yet those who were broken, outcast, and forgotten about, they accepted and believed. If we aren't careful, we begin to look like the older brother, *forgetting* that we were *first* the younger brother. In both cases, they needed love and forgiveness. That's the whole principle. No matter how far low we go, or how high we may excel, we still need Jesus. Without him, we lose our peace, our purpose, and our passion.

What happens when who we have become is no longer who we actually are? One of the traps of perfection is living for people. We develop this sense that if we keep doing what makes people like us, everything will be fine and we subconsciously wait for the praise and recognition. Sometimes, especially if we receive that acknowledgement, we lose complete focus and we compromise. We compromise our callings, our commitments, and our character. When the world rewards us for doing what it would have of us, we forget the One who blessed us with the abilities to do anything. We cannot strive to please the world and please God (Galatians 1:10).

I remember the moment I stopped writing. That moment the fire that lit up inside of me, that affirmed what I would do with my life, was drenched with water so much so it would take years to reignite. I was sitting in my cubicle paging through an exhaustive directory of publishing houses and agents to begin shopping my graduate thesis as a novel ready for publication. I had been out of school for about five or six months and had not touched my novel since I submitted it for completion. The last comment my adviser gave me was, "Publish it. It's so good." But I had not even started the process. As I became settled in the groove of my job and had some distance from completing my novel, I began to feel anxious. Every day that passed I thought about my book and how when I first began my program they told us, "Don't be the writer who leaves their manuscript in their desk." Well, mine is still there.

At that time, I did not have as much faith in my novel as my adviser did. Even now I think about when I will have time to sit with it and make it "really" good (another symptom of perfectionism is procrastination—we wait to produce because we never feel we have reached perfection). In any case, I was comfortable with working a job and not coming home to write because I had a little breathing room. But that did not last long. With my green highlighter and pink rhinestone-heart-shaped bookmark, I began looking for a place to start the process. My boss at the time asked me what I was doing. I explained to her what the book was and the direction I was headed for publishing my work. Her response was, "That can wait. You can make real money doing this. Is your story really that good, anyway?"

The fear of every writer is that no one will think they are a good writer. Even as I have written this book, I have doubted its relevancy, my ability, and whether or not it is even worth it. We fear that our deepest inadequacies will be exposed and we will be considered frauds.

I had already felt pressure to perform at work. No matter how much money came rolling in, how many compliments I received from parents and funders, I never felt that I could perform to the level of acceptancy in that position. To then be discouraged from that which I loved with the worst possible question, a part of me died. Everything I had worked for up until that point felt in vain. I questioned if I had made the right decisions in my academic journey. Was making money what I needed to be focused on now that I was married and had real life adult responsibilities? Because I was good at doing something that I had never done, should I just abandon my dreams and follow this path? Essentially, that is what happened and I lost myself. I compromised living out my purpose for living in what "made sense". I allowed external obligations and priorities to define my life and only when I had time, tried to fit me into my own life. As a result, anytime I tried to write again, it was always seen as a hobby and not an essential. When you let people dictate how you live your life, you allow them to define what is important and what is not.

Pleasing people is a price too heavy to pay. For years I would struggle with getting a job, trusting my employer, trusting in all that God have given me, and dreaming big again. All my degrees, all my accomplishments, all my skills, all my knowledge, none of it was good enough. Before I knew it, that thinking would carry over into my everyday life. I felt like I was failing everyone—my friends, my family, myself, and most importantly, God. I could not hear any of the promises I have shared in this book. I did not believe my life could be more than what it was. I sat in the box the world made for me and adjusted the way I had to breathe in order to survive in such a confined space. Every negative thing said about me stung. I became closed off, guarded, and the sensitivity God made uniquely mine was hardened and numb. I sat down on my hands, the vehicle through which God had blessed me to share with the world all that he deposited in me. I shut off my brain, and I began to question even that which was common sense.

That is how the enemy works. Not just with our gifts and talents, but with every role we take in life. As a woman, a wife, a mother, a daughter, a sister, a friend. Add on race, add on religion, add on occupation, add on education. Are you "woke" enough for your race and culture? Are you too "woke?" Are you holy enough for your fellow church members? Are you too holy for lost souls? Are you feminine enough for women? Are your thoughts and beliefs feminist enough for other women? Do you care about black men as much as you do black women? What do you have all those degrees for if you cannot get a job? Why spend so much money on school? Why serve a God that would let you go through all of this?

Because God's plan will never take you where His grace won't sustain you.

Working on my second master's degree, sorting through thoughts and feelings of inadequacies, I was at a place not one aspect of my identity would accept. As a black woman, you are supposed to be able to take care of yourself. As an educated woman, you are supposed to have a good paying job with benefits. As a Christian woman, you are not supposed to doubt. But I was exactly all of that. Yet through personal decisions and attacks of the enemy, God allowed me to enter a space of total and complete reliance on Him. Each time I thought I surrendered, a new test came and God continued to mold me into maturity. Relationships that had been strained, God said, "it's time to restore." Neglected hurts and pains, it is time to address those. Feelings of inadequacies and negative self-talk, it is time to stop that.

In spite of all that I was experiencing inside, God continued to show me that He held me right in the palm of His hand and He was working everything out for my good. In Chapter 1 I shared how motherhood hit me like a boulder. If there was ever one thing I was always certain of, I knew I would not fail at being a mother. But the dream of motherhood is far from the reality.

When I saw my son crowning, I had no choice but to make decisions for myself without asking for permission. As the doctor called for the NICU team and a spirit of emergency entered my delivery room, I had no room for fear or doubt. After being in labor for almost a full day, reaching a full-term labor, there was no way I would or could believe that my baby would not make it out, living and breathing. I did not care how long or hard I had to push, I would not put my child in distress and he was going to come out breathing and healthy.

Until he wasn't breathing and my world stopped. Suddenly I realized that nothing—not one thing—that I had ever done in life mattered until that moment. And though there were about 20 people in the room, I narrowed in on my son. Watching the doctors patting his back, turning over his blue body and pumping his chest to make him breathe, I whispered, "Come on, baby. You can do this. God, let my baby breathe." Then the cry that stills fills my heart today filled the room and I was instantly a new woman.

Before my son, it was familiar for me to live my life for others. But his entrance in the world made me realize I have someone who needs me to live out the best me. To push past my comfortability, to silence everything and everyone around me and direct my energy and efforts towards what I know, not what others want me to know or how they want me to be. Why? Because that's how I would need to raise him and how can he learn it if I don't live by the same example?

After he was born and we settled into this mommy-son thing, I still had to face all those negative thoughts that I had not yet and those that would come. While there were several, my son taught me the one thing God has been trying to show me for years, "You don't have to be perfect, Mommy. I still love you." I used to take full days to myself once I felt heartbreak or betrayal, shut out the world and internalize everything. Now charged with the responsibility to make sure this beautiful baby grows into a strong healthy man, I could no longer afford to do that.

I had to learn to forgive myself. And not just for any accidents that he may have had. For everything. For being too hard on myself, for not loving myself, for not being gracious or merciful with myself. What he needs from me is to know that sometimes we mess up, but life does not end. We have to get back up, make adjustments, and try again. I have the responsibility of teaching him not just how he has to navigate through his own mistakes, but how to deal with people as they make mistakes—especially women. As the first woman he knows to love, what I teach him about women will affect the way he views and treats women, and that in and of itself is a task I cannot take lightly.

As I began to shake the negativity away from that which surrounded me as a new mother, God blessed me again, with another son, and I knew that served as confirmation, "You are more than enough, Daughter, because you are in me and I am in you." In his natural form, Satan would try to creep in again, but when God has spoken, and you fully believe everything He has told you and begin to walk in that confidence, nothing the enemy sends your way will detour. This is the manifestation of the promise that we are more than conquerors (Romans 8:37).

God gave me the best example of how to be a mother in my mother. She never allowed perfection or what the world expected of her to prohibit her from being everything my sisters and I needed. She made sure we were up and ready for church every Sunday morning, even when other relatives were allowed to do other things—and even when we thought we were too old for her to tell us otherwise. She stressed the importance of education and set higher minimum qualifications for extracurricular activities. As she worked ten to twelve hour shifts, doing labor too rough for any woman's hands, she never allowed what people thought of her to stop her from providing all that we needed, and then some. Even if she never had time to stop and change clothes or get her hair done, she showed up in her work uniform and was always the loudest and proudest, cheering us on. With just one year under my belt, I know that all that I have seen in her is a result of prayer and utter reliance on God. Time and resources not always on her side, she managed to raise her three girls, in the fear of the Lord, into three beautiful young women. I do not say this in pride or arrogance, but her persistence and her dedication to living a life that is pleasing to God and God alone is worth celebrating.

I used to get mad at my mom for always giving money to people. It seemed as if every time she turned around, somebody needed something, and they always came to her. Sometimes, those same people just got through talking about her and she still gave. She used to say, "It's not for the people, I'm doing it for God." I used to say, to myself because I did not want to get hit, "God can help them some other way." I watched as people turned their backs on her, took from her, and talked about her (and us) and she still showed love. I am not yet where my mother is, but now I know her heart and her intentions have always been to please God. Maybe the money she gave could have been saved. Maybe she could have bought herself some of the "finer things" in life. Just maybe, she would not have to work so hard.

But it is not about what I think, or anyone else. If you ask her, she will say she is abundantly blessed. "Not all blessings come in the form of money, and seeing you guys happy and thriving, and being able to help people, that is enough for me."

And there lies the key to unlocking the yoke.

Contentment (Philippians 4:11-13), that is the anecdote to the need for perfection. Not by any power of our own, but through Christ Jesus.

It is not a matter of settling. It is not a matter of getting walked over. It is not a matter of letting people use and abuse you. It is about understanding God's perfect will for your life. It is about recognizing the seasons and allowing God to direct you through them. It is about knowing God's voice and answering to Him, in everything we do. To do so puts you in place for God to mature you, complete you, and make you whole, in Him.

Proverbs 3:5 teaches us trust in the Lord with all of our hearts and not to lean on our own understanding. Following Christ does not mean you will always have a map with clearly outlined routes that avoid detours and make you aware of rest stops. Following Christ means you sit in the driver seat, but you let Jesus take the wheel, and you trust that wherever He is taking you is where you need to be. He paid the price for perfection so that we would not have to. All He asks for in return is our hearts.

Giving my heart to God, completely, allowed me to recognize how any wrong done against me would be turned around for my favor. I was able to release my need to control every aspect of my life because I began to trust that even when I cannot see past today, He knows my whole future. I applied for jobs—both well-paying and minimum wage. Not one door would open. Then God had my full attention. "Just do what I tell you to do." I could not plan out ten steps. My life became a "one step at a time" journey and by such, a walk in faith I had never experienced before.

There may be something God is trying to tell you. Maybe you have been praying for the same thing over and over yet you are getting the same result. Perhaps God wants you to change your request. Maybe He is trying to teach you something in the season you are in because you will need it for what He has next. We get hung up on what we want when God is trying to show us what He has for us. Take a leap of faith, surrender your will to His, and allow Him to show you His great and mighty power.

The Power

of Perfection

> *"God, make me so uncomfortable*
> *that I will do the very thing I fear."*
> — Ruby Dee

One of my all-time favorite movies is *Remember the Titans*. My love for football, the Temptations, Denzel Washington, and happy endings made this story a sure fit to rise to the top of my favorites list. But there is a subtle element in this story that intrigued me. The setting is Alexandra, Virginia, 1971. T.C. Williams High School was about to desegregate and have both black and white students playing on the same football field. As a part of the integration, Coach Boone, played by the master Denzel Washington, was hired as the head coach of T.C. Williams Football team—a team who was already under the leadership Coach Yoast. Coach Boone, an African American man, given the job of Coach Yoast, a white man, inevitably caused havoc in the community.

Coach Yoast was on his way to the High School Football Hall of Fame and started to search for head coaching positions at other schools. The white players, however, refused to play for the school if Yoast was not their coach. Out of loyalty, and maybe a little pride, Yoast stayed and Boone gave him the position of Assistant Coach/Offensive Coordinator. Before the season began, Boone was made privy to some insider information—he could not lose one game or he would be fired, and Yoast would be reinstated as the head coach. Coach Boone had moved his wife and two girls with him to coach that football team. The Black people of that community filled his front yard, excited that they would have a black coach and their boys would have the opportunity to play. The news that he had to have a perfect season became Coach Boone's driving force throughout the duration of the film. He never shared the information with the coaching staff or the team, but he made them all aware that losing was not an option through his coaching methods and tactics.

Of the coaching staff, he is toughest on the players—even the coaches think he is crazy. As the team wins game after game, Boone not only has to deal with the opposition from the other teams, he has to somehow keep his team from hating and hurting each other because of the racism they are accustomed to. Coach Boone is pictured vomiting before the start of one game and later is seen showing clear signs of skepticism towards Coach Yoast. The referees were evidently paid off to ensure the Titans lost that game, and there was absolutely nothing Boone could do about it, and the fear of losing it all was out of his control.

Though Boone was primarily functioning from the desperation and necessity to have a perfect season, he taught those boys who otherwise hated each other how to be brothers. But when the systems are stacked against you, sometimes you need help. Yoast had to step in. His Hall of Fame induction was on the line. He knew that if the Titans continued to win under Boone, they would pull his nomination. For the first half of that game, Yoast allowed the faulty penalties against his team, though cinematically it is revealed that he was struggling with that decision. During halftime, Yoast admits that he had to have a change of heart towards Boone, too. It was never just about football. It became about family.

With the two coaches now working together towards the same common goal, benefitting from each other's strengths, the Titans went on to win the championship and completed a perfect season. But what makes the story great is not the football victory. *Remember the Titans* shows how love and unity can heal and turn around for the better that which otherwise seems impossible.

Many of us, like Coach Boone, go on through life keeping things to ourselves that we feel no one else can handle. Sometimes we do not feel like we have any other choice. We feel alone, neglected, misunderstood, or even ostracized. We make up in our minds, "that's too much for them to know," or, "I got it—I don't need any help." We end up overcompensating and overextending, sometimes to the point of sickness. I have shared personal stories with you as to how doing such has affected my life. Not until I began to let go of all the baggage I was carrying was I able to really start living a full, complete life.

Sometimes, that which hurts us becomes so much a part of our identity, to let it go means to lose a part of ourselves. Our pain, our anger, our anxiety, our fear, our doubt—all of these can become so ingrained into the fabric of who we are that we would not even know how to move forward without them. Because we have become accustomed to living with them, we made a permanent room for them to stay in and letting go would mean something else would have to replace the emptiness. Our biggest fear is that the replacement will be worse than what was there in the first place. At least with the original pain (or whatever your yoke might be), we have learned how to manage it. Something new would be more than we could handle. We hardly ever think that the space can be filled with something good because only that which we *know* is what we rely on. Sons who never want to be their fathers carry everything their father was not with them ever day of their lives. Daughters whose mothers failed to meet the mark wear the disappointment everyday of their lives. Broken hearts lean upon their brokenness as a defense mechanism to never love again. Addicts stay addicted. The lonely stay lonely. The angry stay angry. We do not know how to healthily move on.

Forgiveness, reconciliation, and moving on are all elements of a healthy life, though the hardest to attain. While sitting in a class on racial reconciliation in the church and community, I learned that the path to true forgiveness has always been one with which we—mankind, human beings—struggle. If that were not true, the topic of forgiveness would not be repeated as much as it is in the Bible. I developed a need for perfection through my unwillingness and inability to forgive. Each time something affected me, I did not deal with it; I swept my problems underneath a rug until the rug disappeared into the mighty pile of dust and there was nowhere else for me to sweep. I had to tackle every issue and forgive even that which was not asked to be forgiven (and I'm still forgiving). I had to learn to release myself from the chains of unforgiveness so that I may see myself as the new creation God said I am. I had to understand that falling short did not equate to failing, and I could only reach that point through complete and total surrender.

I told you that contentment was the anecdote to perfection. Well, forgiveness is the prescription. It is far from easy, particularly since the one who has been offended is usually the one who initiates reconciliation. Reconciliation is even harder to attain because the offender has to admit their wrong doing in order for the offended to ever begin to heal. And moving on, well. Most relationships will never go back to what they were, particularly those in which one party refuses to take ownership of their actions or words, and how they affected the other party. Sometimes in reconciliation we have to learn how to be in relationship in a new way, if being in relationship matters. Some ties we will be okay with letting go—and sometimes that is necessary. Others, we must take the time not to rebuild what was there, but to start all over.

A classmate of mine defined moving on after reconciliation as such: "It's just like someone who suffered from a stroke. They may be able to walk, speak, and move again, but it will never be the same way. Through rehabilitation and time, the person will be restored, but they will never be the person they were before the stroke." The magnitude of some of the situations we face that lead to brokenness can feel like a physical infirmity because the condition of our hearts change, one way or the other.

Are you willing to let go of some things, or even people? Are you willing to start anew with others? Forgiving is uncomfortable. We feel as if we are betraying ourselves, or the people with whom we associate ourselves. It can feel as if others "got over" on us, and we carry the fear of appearing weak. Our pride, self-respect, and identity all rest upon knowing we did not let that person, or those people, get away with hurting us. We cut people off. We make them pay over and over and over again for the same mistakes. We hold the past as ransom for any present or future missteps. We do not know how to let go.

Forgiveness is not easy, nor pretty. One day, after struggling to pray because my mind kept making up scenarios for me to lose my mind and let out a whole lot of things I had no business saying, I sat and cried for what felt like hours. During those hours, I did not even have enough strength to pray on my knees. I laid flat out on the floor, weeping, asking God to free me from my own mind. I did not want to be the person I was playing in my own head. I did not want to hurt people because I had been hurt. I did not want to say things I would have to apologize for. Most importantly, I did not want to lose the relationships at hand because of what could have come out of *my* mouth. Whatever I had to do, I was ready to do it. Until He said, "You have to forgive first." I did not want that answer. I wanted God to tell me that He would get them for hurting me, His daughter. I wanted Him to tell me to cut the ties and that He would understand if I never spoke to them again. But He told me to make the first move.

I moved from my prostrate position to fetal position. Still crying, I asked God to hold me. I prayed for His presence to fill the room so that I could feel Him. Not in a heightened emotional understanding of His presence, I needed a tangible feeling. I needed His comfort because nothing else would have sufficed. As I focused on entering His presence, my mind shifted from focusing on my problem to focusing on my Problem Solver. A warmth fell over me. I rested my head and began to release. Some people turn to music. Some to self-help books, church, cooking, hiking, baking, writing, or whatever other outlet that works for them. I have tried most of these too (still have to do better with the hiking—I'll get there, eventually). But what I found is that even though these avenues help temporarily, there is only one thing that stitches up my wounds and provides me with detailed instructions for future care, and that is the Word of God.

I said it before, Christianity was never meant to be a set of rules that would lead us closer to God. Yes, He gave us commandments to follow and instructions on how to model our lives after that of Christ, but He did not ever tell us we had to walk alone. After Jesus' ascension, He promised to send us a Comforter to be with us, always (John 14:16). Most people forget about the Holy Spirit. In fact, Jesus says the world will not receive Him because they cannot see Him, but for those of us who have asked for Him to dwell in us, He will be a present help (John 14:17). When I am completely lost, cannot find my way, cannot tell my night from day, I know I have the Holy Spirit to guide me to and through the word of God to find my comfort.

You cannot and will not always find what you need from God in many other places though He does speak to people in more ways than the Bible. Sometimes it is in wise counsel from a loved one, sometimes it is through a work of art, literature, or music. Sometimes it is in nature, where He reminds us just how big He is. But there is something about the Word of God that cannot be matched.

I believe it is the power of His perfection.

We do not have to look any further than Jesus. On the cross He bore every sin, every hurt, every pain, and every heartbreak. He then invited us to live in Him and He in us. And the same power that rose Him up from the grave, He made it available to you and me (Ephesians 1:19-20).

We, therefore, have no need to continue in bondage. He is a God who keeps His promises, and though they are many, He will never fail.

If you find yourself having a rough time in life, and therefore a tough time trusting in God, be reminded of these things:

> Genesis 28:15: *"I am with you and will watch over you wherever you go."*

> Deuteronomy 31:8: *"the Lord himself goes before you and will be with you; he will never leave you nor forsake you. Do not be afraid; do not be discouraged."*

> Nehemiah 8:10: *"The joy of the Lord is your strength."*

> Psalm 9:9-10: *"The Lord is a refuge for the oppressed, a stronghold in times of trouble. Those who know your name trust in you, for you, Lord, have never forsaken those who seek you."*

> Psalm 23:4: *"Even though I walk through the darkest valley, I will fear no evil. For you are with me. Your rod and your staff, they comfort me."*

> Psalm 27:1: *"The Lord is my light and my salvation—whom shall I fear? The Lord is the stronghold of my life—of whom shall I be afraid?"*

> Psalm 34:18: *"The Lord is close to the broken hearted and saves those who are crushed in spirit."*

Psalm 46:10: *"Be still and know that I am God."*

Psalm 50:15: *"And call on me in the day of trouble and I will deliver you, and you will honor me."*

Psalm 107: 13-16: *"Then they cried to the Lord in their trouble, and he saved them from their distress. He brought them out of darkness, the utter darkness and broke away their chains. Let them give thanks to the Lord for his unfailing love and his wonderful deeds for mankind, for he breaks down gates of bronze and cuts through bars of iron."*

Proverbs 3:5-6: *"Trust in the Lord with all your heart and lean not on your own understanding; in all your ways submit to him, and he will make your paths straight."*

Isaiah 40:29-31: *"He gives strength to the weary and increases the power of the weak. Even youths grow tired and weary, and young men stumble and fall, but those who hope in the Lord will renew their strength. They will soar on wings like eagles; they will run and not grow weary, they will walk and not faint."*

Isaiah 43:2: *"When you pass through the waters, I will be with you; and when you pass through the rivers, they will not sweep over you. When you walk through the fire, you will not be burned; the flames will not set you ablaze.*

Isaiah 54:10: *"Though the mountains be shaken and the hills be removed, yet my unfailing love for you will not be shaken nor my covenant of peace be removed."*

Isaiah 54:17: *"no weapon forged against you will prevail, and you will refute every tongue that accuses you. This is the heritage of the servants of the Lord, and this is their vindication from me."*

Isaiah 58:6: *"Is not this the kind of fasting I have chosen: to loose the chains of injustice and untie the cords of the yoke, to set the oppressed free and break every yoke?"*

Jeremiah 29:11: *"'For I know the plans I have for you,' declares the Lord, 'plans to prosper you and not to harm you, plans to give you hope and a future.'"*

Lamentations 3:24-26: *"I say to myself, 'The Lord is my portion; therefore, I will wait for him.' The Lord is good to those whose hope is in him, to the one who seeks him; it is good to wait quietly for the salvation of the Lord."*

Matthew 6:33: *"But seek first his kingdom and his righteousness, and all these things will be given to you as well."*

Mark 11:24: *"Therefore I tell you, whatever you ask for in prayer, believe that you have received it, and it will be yours."*

John 8:36: *"So if the Son sets you free, you will be free indeed."*

Romans 8:28: *"And we know that in all things God works for the good of those who love him, who have been called according to his purpose."*

Romans 10:9-10: *"If you declare with your mouth, 'Jesus is Lord,' and believe in your heart that God raised him from the dead, you will be saved. For it is with your heart that you believe and are justified, and it is with your mouth that you profess your faith and are saved."*

2 Corinthians 12:8-10: *"Three times I pleaded with the Lord to take it away from me. But he said to me, 'My grace is sufficient for you, for my power is made perfect in weakness.' Therefore, I will boast all the more gladly about my weaknesses, so that Christ's power may rest on me. That is why, for Christ's sake, I delight in weaknesses, in insults, in hardships, in persecutions, in difficulties. For when I am weak, then I am strong.*

Philippians 4:6-7: *"Do not be anxious about anything, but in every situation, by prayer and petition, with thanksgiving, present your requests to God. And the peace of God, which transcends all understanding, will guard your hearts and your minds in Christ Jesus."*

James 4:7: *"Submit yourselves, then, to God. Resist the*

devil, and he will flee from you."

1 John 1:9: *"If we confess our sins, he is faithful and just and will forgive us our sins and purify us from all un-righteousness."*

From beginning to the end, God is always there. He wants what is best for you. We never have to be nor feel alone.

I know I just gave you a lot of scriptures, and the truth is, there are more that may speak directly to you. It is my prayer that as you seek God's face, He will speak to you through His word. Whether it is through a scripture I have provided or one that you find on your own, may His peace find you and His love make you whole.

Before I end this book, I want you to know that this journey will not be easy. Even as I write my final thoughts, I am convicted of things I need to take to the Lord and leave there. Some of these pages were written with full tears in my eyes, others under a blanket of anxiety. The important matter is, though, they are done. Life will teach you that sometimes our suffering does not end. Sometimes, we have to learn to live with our struggles, even when we grow weary. That does not take away from them being real, but it adds to the story of the magnificence of who God made you to be. You do not have to wait for perfect conditions to start living your full life. As long as you choose to give yourself a chance, you are doing more than enough.

Your yoke can be strong, but Jesus tells us in Matthew 11:28-30, "Come to me, all you who are weary and burdened, and I will give you rest. Take my yoke upon you and learn from me, for I am gentle and humble in heart, and you will find rest for your souls. For my yoke is easy and my burden is light."

It is my prayer that you find rest, and may the Spirit of God keep you lifted as you release the yoke.

Afterword

Striving towards worldly perfection has made my life one of which I look back and am continually reminded to thank God for His grace, His mercy, and His favor. I've taken my eyes off of His purpose for my life and tried to lead myself on this journey. Achieving perfection to the worlds standards has at times been my motivation, and others been my biggest obstacle. Now it most definitely serves as my greatest testimony, because everything the enemy tried to use against me to harm me, God turned it around for my good.

What is holding you back? Maybe you are an overcoming perfectionist, like me, but perhaps your yoke has been/is something else. I invite you to write a letter to yourself on the following pages. Allow yourself the freedom to be honest about what you're missing in life and how YOU might in fact be the reason why you have yet to obtain all that God has already prepared for you. But before you begin, pray this prayer with me:

"Dear God,

Thank you for your love. Thank you for sending your Son to free me from the evil snares of this world. Thank you for pouring your grace and mercy over my life, especially during the times I failed to acknowledge you. Lord, forgive me of the sins I have committed towards you. Wash me clean of all negative and hurtful thoughts and actions I have told and committed against myself and others. Heal me from the pain I have caused myself and heal those to whom I have caused pain. Help me to see myself the way you see me. Help me to view others as you see them. Teach me to walk in the ways of your will for my life. From this day forward, may my goal be to live in the freedom that Jesus' life gave me. May you break the yokes and chains that would keep me bound from living totally and completely free in you. I surrender my life and my will to you.

In Jesus' Name I Pray,
Amen."

Do not let the number of pages intimidate you. Write what you can, whatever is in your heart. If you run out of space, I encourage you to finish in a journal or notebook where you can keep this letter safe. Whenever you feel the tug of the enemy pulling you back into bondage, break out this letter and remind yourself that through the power of the Spirit of God, you have been released from that yoke.

Love Always.

Stay Connected

Blog
www.acjacobswrites.com

Email
acjacobswrites@gmail.com

Instagram
@acjacobswrites

Facebook
@acjacobswrites

Twitter
@acjacobswrites

51324591R00071

Made in the USA
San Bernardino, CA
19 July 2017